MANAGEMENT BY OBJECTIVES

A SELF-INSTRUCTIONAL APPROACH

WILLIAM C. GIEGOLD
Virginia Polytechnic Institute and State University

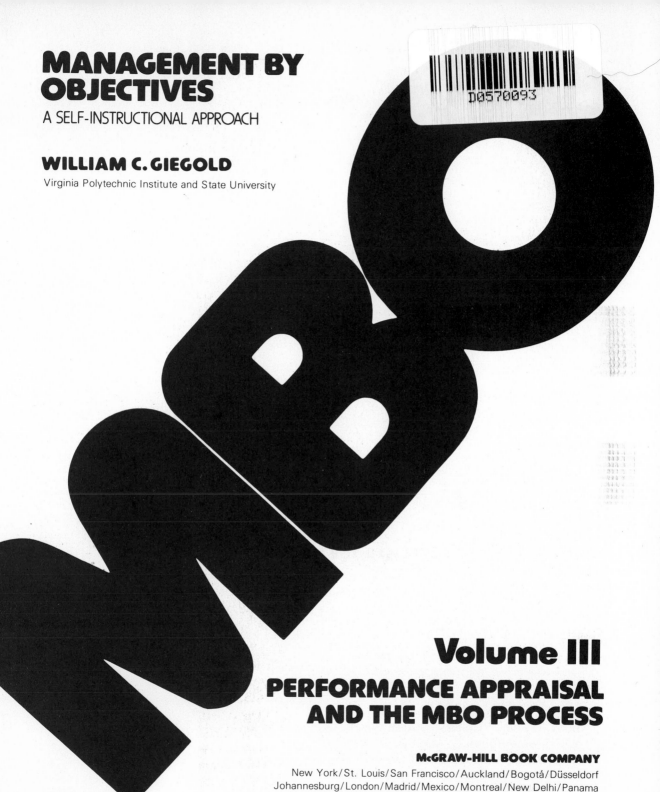

Volume III
PERFORMANCE APPRAISAL AND THE MBO PROCESS

McGRAW-HILL BOOK COMPANY

New York/St. Louis/San Francisco/Auckland/Bogotá/Düsseldorf
Johannesburg/London/Madrid/Mexico/Montreal/New Delhi/Panama
Paris/São Paulo/Singapore/Sydney/Tokyo/Toronto

Library of Congress Cataloging in Publication Data

Giegold, William C
    Management by objectives.

      CONTENTS: v. 1. Strategic planning and the MBO process. — v. 2.
Objective setting and the MBO process. — v. 3. Per-
formance appraisal and the MBO process.
      1. Management by objectives — Collected works.
I. Title.
HD30.12.G53   658.4   78–14764
ISBN 0-07-023190-7

**PERFORMANCE APPRAISAL AND THE MBO PROCESS
VOLUME III**

MANAGEMENT BY OBJECTIVES: A Self-Instructional Approach

 2 3 4 5 6 7 8 9 0 DODO 7 8 3 2 1 0 9

This book was set in Univers by Allen Wayne Technical Corp.
The editors were Robert G. Manley and John Hendry;
the designer was Anne Canevari Green;
the production supervisor was Jeanne Selzam.
R. R. Donnelley & Sons Company was printer and binder.

CONTENTS

iii

PREFACE

This is the third volume of a three-volume series entitled *Management by Objectives: A Self-Instructional Approach.* The series is intended to achieve the following objectives:

1. To facilitate one's understanding of the management system known as Management by Objectives, or MBO for short.
2. To identify and describe the elements which make up the MBO system and the interpersonal skills which enhance the chances of its successful implementation.
3. To give the reader an opportunity to develop the required skills and to experience some of the problems and pitfalls that may arise in implementing MBO.
4. To help the reader develop a management system which adapts the general principles of MBO to the specific needs of his or her organization.

Each volume may be used independently of the others by those readers or organizations whose needs lie predominantly in the areas covered by only one or two of the books. In this volume we cover the performance appraisal process, as described below. Volume I concentrates on the strategic planning process, and Volume II deals with the processes of setting objectives and formulating action plans.

The three volumes are self-instructional since they allow an individual reader, by completing the exercises, to apply the principles of MBO to his or her own organization or job, and thus have a firsthand knowledge of the problems and pitfalls one may encounter when introducing MBO into an organization. If you are a manager, completion of this self-study will give you the ability and confidence to install such a system in your own component, with little or no outside assistance. The *Leader's Manual* which accompanies the series gives further help to any reader who takes on the responsibility of conducting MBO training for others in an organization—employees or coworkers—in a group setting.

This volume, like each of the others in the series, begins with a general overview of the MBO system. It then turns to the performance appraisal process, which completes the MBO cycle. Performance appraisal provides management with the information needed to reexamine its directions and fine-tune its objectives, in addition to measuring how well things are going. It is a dialogue between management and employees that not only tells the employee how well he or she is doing, but also helps managers keep abreast of what is happening both inside and outside the organization.

Your ability as a manager to conduct such a dialogue with your employees (and with your boss) is crucial to the success of implementing MBO in your organization. In fact, we will go further and state categorically that a breakdown in the managerial control system, of which employee performance review is an essential part, is a prime cause of management failure. In a sense, this can be the most important volume in the series for you, the manager. The principles of human interaction and motivation that we cover here will be valuable in whatever organizational context you operate, now and in the future, whether or not your organization adopts the "total MBO" approach.

The primary skill that you will develop in this volume is the skill of interacting with others. This skill cannot be acquired to any appreciable extent by self-study alone. We recommend that you find an associate with whom you can practice working through some of the situations presented here. Other more complex situations, requiring a leader or facilitator, are provided in the *Leader's Manual.* You may wish to consider using them in training your subordinate managers in interaction skills.

You may also need answers to questions about performance appraisal that have arisen out of your experiences to date—questions about the cause-and-effect relationship between appraisal and performance, the role of compensation in an MBO system, the proper use of "personality" as a topic in an appraisal discussion, and so on. We will let you compare your answers to questions like these with our own suggestions. By blending your experiences and thoughts with ours, you will arrive at a better understanding of (and a much more secure feeling about) this somewhat controversial but crucially important management tool—performance appraisal.

No book in a field as broad as management is the work of the writer alone. We acknowledge the immense contributions of forerunners whose works are cited herein, as well as many unnamed others whose thoughts provided the springboard for this work. A special debt of gratitude is due to Mike Crump of Syracuse University's School of Management, who conceived the idea for this series but who unfortunately was unable to play his rightful role in making it come to pass.

We thank Frank Mahoney, Art Kirn, and C. C. Schmidt for their painstaking reviews of the manuscript and their helpful suggestions, many of which they will find incorporated within. Project manager John Hendry has shown great patience and skill in keeping the author's feet on the ground. He and the McGraw-Hill staff—Bob Manley, Bob Leap, Anne Green, and the many copy editors, artists, compositors, and others who have put a bit of themselves into these books—would command any author's admiration and respect.

Finally, to Irma, who typed the manuscripts and whose editing of the raw material made the job much easier for the professsionals, goes more than thanks for her loving support throughout.

William C. Giegold

UNIT 1

INTRODUCTION

AN OVERVIEW OF THE MANAGEMENT BY OBJECTIVES SYSTEM

The phrase "management by objectives," or MBO for short, has become a part of the language of management throughout the world. Managers, supervisors, and others in responsible positions at every level in almost every type and size of organization, from churches to the military, and from the multinational corporation to the family-owned hardware store, are on speaking acquaintance with the concept. It has appeared under several names — results-oriented management, management by objectives and results (MBO/R), work planning and review, "planagement," and management by agreement, to list a few. The names reveal the particular emphasis or bias of their authors. One stresses the planning aspects. Another emphasizes the give-and-take by which bosses and subordinates agree on their mutual goals. Others reflect merely their authors' dissatisfaction with the ability of the original name — MBO — to convey the full meaning and purpose of the management system to which it refers.

Whatever its title, the principles of this system remain the same, as valid as they were when originally proposed a quarter of a century ago. They compose the most rational system of "total management" yet developed. In spite of this, unfortunately, the potential of the system remains today largely as promise rather than realization. The ranks of those who have "tried it" in a superficial or halfhearted way and been disappointed far outnumber those who have understood it and had the will to submit to its demands. Those who have done so can testify to its merits. They can also testify to the fact that it is a *demanding* system of management.

In this guided tour of the system we will stop frequently and let you experience for yourself the extent of the commitment you must make to excellence in the profession of management when you opt for MBO. Whether you are the top person in your organization, a first-line manager, or not yet appointed to your first management job—and whether or not your organization formally adopts an MBO system—you can become a much more effective manager by putting to work on the job what you practice in this series of books.

A DEFINITION OF MANAGE-MENT BY OBJECTIVES

"Management by objectives" has been defined by George Odiorne as:

 . . . a management process *whereby the supervisor and the subordinate, operating under a* clear definition *of the common* goals and priorities *of the organization established by* top management, jointly *identify the individual's major* areas of responsibility *in terms of the* results expected *of him or her, and* use *these* measures *as guides for operating the unit and assessing the* contributions *of each of its members.*[1]

Written in the early days of MBO, this definition has retained its currency and covers very concisely the essential features of this

[1]George S. Odiorne, *Management by Objectives: A System of Managerial Leadership* (New York, Pitman, 1965), pp. 55-56.

system of management. It is rich in meanings which do not reveal themselves until it has been examined word for word. We have emphasized several key words and phrases, and point out their significance below. In this volume and the others in this series, we will expand on each of these points to provide a thorough knowledge of the principles of MBO and how to put them to work in your organization. We will also relate them to your effectiveness as an individual, on and off the job.

The key words are these:

process — MBO, like management itself, is a continuing activity, not a "campaign," a "program," or a onetime installation project which when completed can produce results on its own. It is an endless cyclical group of interrelated management activities embodying all the conventional management functions of planning, organizing, directing, and controlling. We show it as a flowchart in Fig. 1, and will explain the steps later in this unit.

clear definition of goals — This is the thrust which the name MBO implies. Clearly defined goals or objectives provide the focus of effort which is required for the most efficient use of resources. ("Goal" and "objective" are interchangeable terms. We will primarily use the latter throughout this series.)

priorities — Objectives are not enough to ensure organizational or individual effectiveness. One must be sure that the most important objectives are tackled first, and a system for establishing priorities is a vital link in the overall process.

top management — If the clear definition of goals and priorities begins at the very top, the system achieves its fullest potential, since all parts of the organization set their sights on the same overall target. Top management also plays a continuing role in emphasizing the need for organizational improvement. The single strongest motivating factor in a successful MBO system is top management's support of and demand for the degree of management effort required by MBO.

jointly — In the MBO effort, the process of joint objective setting by the manager and the employee is the key to obtaining full cooperation and acceptance by employees. This same process is also the means by which the full knowledge and creative potential of the employee are brought to bear on the improvement needs of the organization.

areas of responsibility—Every position or job must exist for a purpose well defined in relationship to the needs of the organization. This relationship is established through the *key results areas* (KRAs) of the organization, which determine the job responsibilities most important to overall needs, and guide the search for meaningful objectives. (We will have more to say about key results areas in due course.)

results expected—The apparent emphasis on objectives in MBO may seem to neglect the purpose for which the whole effort is designed: *to produce results which would not otherwise be*

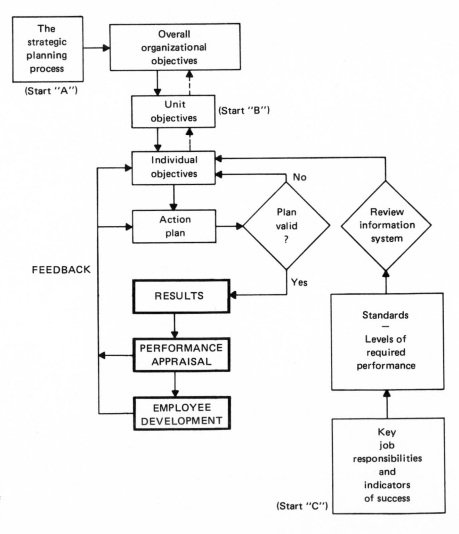

FIGURE 1
A flowchart of
the MBO process.

achieved. Stating the expectations of management is a most potent way of communicating with employees. Expressing these expectations in terms of the needed results replaces vague exhortations or, worse yet, the silence which communicates management's acceptance of the status quo.

use ("to use," an *active* verb) — The establishment of objectives at all levels in an organization is an important part of the MBO system, but in too many cases it has been mistaken for the *purpose* of the system. A campaign is mounted, individuals and managers at all levels strain mightily to produce volume upon volume of objectives — and the results are placed on the shelf, to be removed only to demonstrate proudly that "we have MBO."

measures — Unless the objectives are *used* to measure progress and the measurements are then used to make adjustments and corrections which *accelerate* progress, MBO remains static and sterile, rather than becoming the dynamic and productive system it is designed to be.

contributions — MBO encourages the contribution of every individual to the overall objectives of the organization, measures each contribution, and provides the basis for rewards in proportion.

THE PURPOSE OF MBO: IMPROVED EFFECTIVENESS

A key word left out of Odiorne's description, and the primary reason for considering MBO for your organization, is "improvement." What we are working on here is improvement in both organizational and individual effectiveness. The most productive way to look at an objective is as an *improvement need* relative to the situation as it is now or as it is forecast to become unless deliberate action is taken. We stress this word and this concept of an objective because of the tendency to set objectives which merely document what the organization is already doing. Such an approach may satisfy all the formalities, but it turns MBO into a ritual rather than a thrust toward improvement.

A second reason for considering MBO, as we have suggested, is that it provides guidance in the conduct of the management process itself. As a framework for organizing managerial thought and activity, MBO satisfies all the needs of a manager who is attempting to follow the prescriptions of management authorities such as Peter Drucker. Drucker's concept of the management job requires first answering the question "What are the purposes and nature of our organization, and what should they be?" Next, clear objectives and goals are established, with priorities and measures of performance. Then a climate is created in which employees exercise self-correction and self-control by maintaining a continuing audit of the results and the objectives themselves, and adjusting their efforts as needed.

The correspondence between Odiorne's definition of MBO and Drucker's summary of the total management job is striking. It identifies MBO as a *system of management* rather than, in the view often taken, as a management tool or technique to be superimposed on "everything else that we are already doing."

THE MBO SYSTEM: A BRIEF DESCRIPTION

Figure 1 illustrates the system in flowchart form. The highlighted portions are covered in this third volume of the three-volume series. Volume I deals with the strategic-planning process; Vol. II is concerned with objective setting and action planning.

Here, step by step, is how the whole thing works:

The strategic planning activity   MBO does not "start with objectives," but with strategic planning. (See starting point A in Fig. 1.) This process is necessary to determine what kinds of objectives are compatible with the purposes, strengths, and resources of the organization. Before attempting to set organizational objectives,

It is important to resist the tendency to set objectives which merely document what the organization is already doing. (© Brilliant Enterprises, 1974.)

TO BE SURE OF HITTING THE TARGET,

SHOOT FIRST

AND, WHATEVER YOU HIT, CALL IT THE TARGET.

strategic planning answers two major questions: "Why are we here?" and "Who are we?" Only after these questions have been answered can we intelligently ask the third question: "Where are we going?" Answering the first two questions involves self-analysis by the organization, competitive and environmental analysis, and a series of comparisons—with *competitors' achievements* and with *our own potential*—to determine organizational strengths and weaknesses. This analysis, initiated by top management, determines how resources can best be concentrated and deployed, a maneuver we call "strategy selection." Strategic planning and its use in selecting organizational objectives are the subject of Vol. I.

Although strategic planning is initiated by top management for the organization as a whole, the type of thinking it entails is equally important for a smaller component of the organization, and even for the individual employee or manager. In Vol. I we discuss at some length how these principles can be applied to a person's job or career strategy.

Overall organizational objectives   These are the short-range and long-range targets for organizational improvement established by the highest level of management. They are the basis for much of the objective setting done at lower levels in the organization, as each unit or component determines its contribution to the overall objective.

Overall organizational objectives, like all objectives in the MBO system, have three main purposes. These are to:

1.   Function as records of commitments made by their authors
2.   Serve as a yardstick for measuring progress
3.   Act as positive motivators of achievement

To be fully functional, an objective must be prepared with a number of stringent requirements continually in mind. Some of the more obvious are clarity, specificity, measurability, and, surprisingly perhaps, achievability. High-sounding, ambitious objectives that exceed their author's capability, resources, or authority weaken an MBO system by destroying its credibility. We will cover the requirements of sound objectives later in this unit.

Unit objectives   All units are called on to contribute to the organization's objectives, as noted above. This does not mean, however, that the component must wait to be directed, nor does it mean that the component cannot initiate objectives based on the firsthand view of the situation which only its members enjoy. The reverse (dashed) arrow in Fig. 1 signifies the unit's influence on the overall organizational objectives and its responsibility to feed its firsthand knowledge into the system.

While the strategic planning process is the ideal starting point (A on the flowchart) for an organization adopting an MBO system, a single unit may be used as the starting point for a pilot effort (point B). If this alternative is taken, there is still a need to assure conformance with overall organizational needs, and to think strategically about the resource deployment of the unit before deciding on its objectives.

Individual objectives   On the flowchart (Fig. 1) individual objectives are the focal point for much of the flow of information and action in the MBO process. The individual is the ultimate contributor to overall organizational objectives as well as to unit objectives. Note that, as the reverse arrow indicates, the individual also has the opportunity and the responsibility to shape and modify the higher-level objectives. Later in this unit we will describe the other flows which terminate in this block of the diagram.

Figure 2 illustrates how the individual responds to an overall need for profit improvement in a multilevel organization. As the overall targets are considered at successively lower levels, the resulting objectives will normally become much more detailed and narrower in scope.

Note that the arrows depicting the flow of the objective-setting process point in both directions. This indicates the dynamic nature of the process, in which the ideas responding to the overall need flow *up,* while the motivating force for the generation of the nature and size of the total contributions needed flows *down.* The upward flow also implies that the total of manufacturing and other functional contributions must be examined closely against the overall need in order to determine the adequacy of the

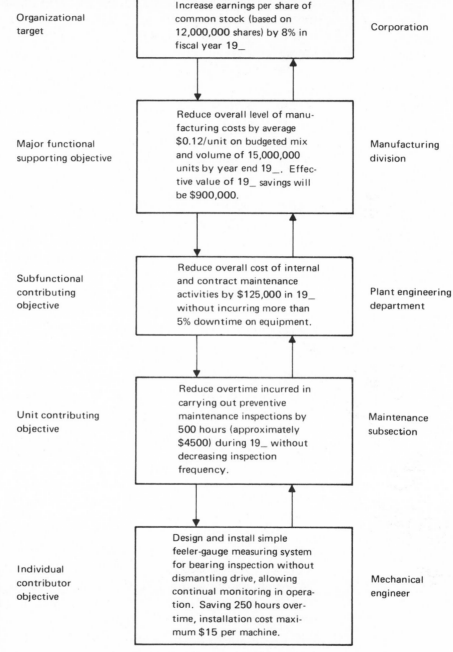

Organizational target	Increase earnings per share of common stock (based on 12,000,000 shares) by 8% in fiscal year 19_	Corporation
Major functional supporting objective	Reduce overall level of manufacturing costs by average $0.12/unit on budgeted mix and volume of 15,000,000 units by year end 19_. Effective value of 19_ savings will be $900,000.	Manufacturing division
Subfunctional contributing objective	Reduce overall cost of internal and contract maintenance activities by $125,000 in 19_ without incurring more than 5% downtime on equipment.	Plant engineering department
Unit contributing objective	Reduce overtime incurred in carrying out preventive maintenance inspections by 500 hours (approximately $4500) during 19_ without decreasing inspection frequency.	Maintenance subsection
Individual contributor objective	Design and install simple feeler-gauge measuring system for bearing inspection without dismantling drive, allowing continual monitoring in operation. Saving 250 hours overtime, installation cost maximum $15 per machine.	Mechanical engineer

FIGURE 2
The increasing detail and narrowing scope of supporting objectives in a five-layer organization.

overall cost reduction effort. For example, if all individual and sub-functional manufacturing contributions only add up to $450,000 of cost reduction available in 19__ from manufacturing, the manufacturing objective itself must be reexamined.

It is also possible, however, that the corporate profit improvement target was set without enough thought to its achievability, or that it relies too heavily on cost reduction rather than on sales volume, pricing, and other contributors to profit improvement. The setting of overall organizational objectives is discussed, together with the strategic planning process, in Vol. 1.

Plan for action   As we will stress later in this unit, the detailed plan for reaching an objective is an essential part of the objective itself. It details who is going to do what, when, and with whose help. The plan fulfills three important functions: it describes how the objective will be reached and therefore enhances the validity and credibility of the objective, it budgets the time and other resources required of those responsible, and it is used for monitoring progress toward the ultimate objective.

Validity of the action plan   Close scrutiny of the action plan itself is one of the best methods for validating an objective—that is, for assuring that it has a high probability of achievement. Such scrutiny determines whether the quality and quantity of the resources assigned to it are adequate. It also serves as a check on the quality of the planning itself. Any major flaws revealed at this point will require a change of plan, a change of objective, or both, as indicated by the decision branch ("no" or "yes") in the flowchart.

There are other opportunities to validate an action plan. One is the joint objective-setting discussion mentioned in Odiorne's definition. This procedure assures that the manager and the employee are jointly committed to achieving the objective. The manager commits his or her effort in helping the employee surmount obstacles and attain success. To arrive at that agreement, the manager first must be convinced of the desirability and validity of the employee's proposed objective. Two heads thus applied to the examination of the proposed objective make more than doubly certain that its conception is sound.

Results   This small single block on the flowchart represents the reason your organization exists — the production of goods or services. Lest we appear to be slighting this most important concern of every organization, we remind you that the primary purpose of everything else we are discussing is the *continual improvement of results* through better planning, direction and feedback.

Performance review   Each employee should continually review and appraise his or her results, and this review and appraisal should be supplemented by periodic formal discussions between manager and employee. These activities breathe life into what otherwise might become a static and nonproductive exercise in planning. The review process consists of:

1.   The day-by-day assessment of progress
2.   The continual problem solving which keeps things moving
3.   Periodic reviews wherein the manager and the employee assess results and replan future efforts, if necessary
4.   The manager's infrequent but regular appraisal of the employee's performance and potential

The first three items are mainly concerned with the progress of the work itself, whereas the fourth is primarily employee-oriented. The first two, concerned with the day-to-day control of the work, are left in the hands of the employee, with help from the manager as needed. The periodic review and the performance appraisal, quarterly and annual respectively, are joint discussions with the manager.

Feedback   The results of the performance review and appraisal process are fed back into the ongoing objective-setting and action planning process, and help determine changes in objectives and plans. Revision of individuals' objectives affect unit objectives as well. Feedback from the employee to the manager during the periodic review discussion may show that the employee needs the manager's help to clear obstacles from the path of progress. (Such efforts often become a part of the manager's personal objectives.) Feedback thus keeps the MBO system responsive to problems, deviations, and the need for corrective effort. The feedback does not stop at the level of the individual and the manager. Inputs from the individual level are often critical to the strategic planning process and the reshaping of overall organizational objectives.

In the MBO process, "feedback" also means the information given to the employee about performance, in both the technical and the human relations aspects of the job. Much of this kind of feedback comes from the manager. For the employee, it fills very important psychological needs for recognition and for knowing "how I'm doing" in the eyes of the boss. It is also important that the employee have access to feedback in the form of reports or other measurement tools that give *direct* information about progress without the intervention of the manager. This kind of feedback allows the employee to exert a maximum of self-control and responsibility on the job.

Employee development   The performance review may indicate that the employee needs further training or other forms of development in order to perform the present job effectively or to prepare for future positions that may be suggested by the performance-and-potential appraisal. The MBO system may become a highly mechanistic form of management unless managers maintain and demonstrate a genuine interest in their employee's personal and professional development. This is essential to the realization of the full benefits the system offers.

We will discuss the potential benefits of both the mechanistic and the employee-centered application of MBO later in this unit, but first the series of processes leading to the individual objectives step in the Fig. 1 flowchart must be explained. These processes are essential prerequisites to the individual objective-setting process. In effect, they represent strategic planning at the "micro" level, focusing on the individual. They are analogous in many respects to the "macro" process of strategy formulation for the organization as a whole.

Individual responsibilities   Each jobholder must have a clear understanding of the reasons for the existence of the job, its key responsibilities, and the priorities each of these responsibilities carries. This may seem a truism, but it is often overlooked. The well-known example of customer service specialists who regard phone calls from customers as interruptions which prevent them from catching up on paperwork illustrates the need to get back to basics — on the part of the manager as well as the specialist!

Lacking (or losing) this perspective on the important contributions the job must provide, the employee may become embroiled in time-consuming activity that contributes little to the desired results. The employee's efforts will tend to become increasingly misdirected unless the relationship between the job and the organizational mission is kept in mind. To avoid this problem, a thorough understanding of the key results areas of the organization is essential. The KRAs are those aspects of total performance in which an organization must continually set and achieve objectives for improvement to preserve its health and assure its growth.

It is also important for every employee to have a model of mature, expert performance — or, more specifically, an indicator of success for each important responsibility, answering the question "How will I know when this part of my job is being done well?" These indicators should be incorporated in the job description or other document defining the job.

Job descriptions are not a new concept. All organizations use them to list the duties of the jobholder, to give information to prospective candidates for the job, and as a guide to selection of the right individual in terms of abilities, experience, and interests. In some cases, the employee may pull his or her own job description out of the files from time to time, and refer to it as a checklist to see whether all the bases are being covered. Managers may refer to the job descriptions of their subordinates at appraisal time to refresh their memories on exactly what each person is supposed to be doing. However, the MBO process requires more than a mere list of the duties which a jobholder is expected to perform from time to time while occupying the position. The inputs from the lower right portion of Fig. 1 (leading to the individual's objectives), which provide the link between the unit or component objectives and what the individual actually contributes, come from a more sophisticated version of the job description than a mere listing of duties.

The position guide, or job description, in the MBO system specifies levels of performance for each duty or responsibility. It indicates the achievement level which a fully trained and mature incumbent would be expected to reach on the job — the ultimate in performance. Obviously, not every incumbent, especially in the first months or even years on the job, can reasonably be expected to achieve these ultimate levels of performance — certainly not if jobs are designed to provide opportunities for growth. Interim levels which *can* be achieved are therefore established to provide shorter-range targets for the new incumbent, since the "impossible dream" may not be the most appropriate motivator for the newcomer. We will illustrate the nature and uses of the MBO job description in Unit 6.

You may question the value of having two sets of targets for the individual. An analogy may be found in long-distance running. For many years, long-distance runners held the 4-minute mile as an "unachievable" but prized goal. Before that elusive record was reached, there were of course many winners along the way. Performances of long-distance runners became steadily more impressive in part because that goal existed. Along the way, however, it is probable that most runners found their real motivation in an attempt to better the fastest previous performance or to knock another second off their own best previous time.

Levels of performance   Establishing levels of performance in the form of standards of excellence — the highest achievements in the field — helps keep in view the opportunities for improvement in the routine, continuing duties of any job. In the rare case, present performance may be at such a masterful level already. Here the standard can act as a baseline for measuring deterioration in performance if it occurs. In any case, the objectives of each individual must be apportioned between the routine and the often more interesting and appealing creative projects. Having a level of ultimate performance as a reminder encourages attention to the routine.

The information system   Measurements of performance are readily established and verified in some cases, but not in others. The expense of time and effort in gathering the data necessary to assess performance against a measurement criterion that was hastily proposed can be great. The capabilities of the existing information system must be examined carefully when you prepare standards. Often information presently available will suggest a form in which the standards can be expressed without generating new data.

In any case, the climate of self-control mentioned earlier requires that the information be made available directly to the employee in a timely fashion. Ideally, the employee is the *first to become aware* of problems and has the maximum opportunity to correct them.

A STARTING POINT FOR INDIVIDUALIZED MBO

When this chain of prerequisite planning processes has been completed, the individual is in a position to select most effectively the objectives pertinent to the job. Once these processes are completed to the mutual satisfaction of manager and employee, the output, usually in the form of a job description of the type described above, should become a *working tool* for both, not merely a part of the permanent organization manual for the unit (which normally just gathers dust in someone's file drawer or bookcase). At the very least it should be used to prepare for the periodic performance appraisal and to guide newcomers on the job.

Preparation of such a detailed job description constitutes a method whereby you, the individual employee or manager, can institute your own test of MBO. We have designated starting point C on the flowchart as the point of entry for the individual. Though it is possible to carry out some of the essential parts of the process yourself, the review of your performance will of course be much less subjective if you enlist the help of your immediate manager. Doing so will also give a broader perspective on organizational KRAs, unit objectives, and other inputs you will need. (It is not necessary to have formal companywide KRAs or objectives in effect. You can generate a reasonable facsimile — enough to serve this limited purpose — in dialogue with your manager.) If you are a manager, you may wish to try this same approach by selecting an employee to conduct the test of the system. If you decide to do this, don't overlook your own responsibilities in making the system work. We have referred to these responsibilities earlier, and will discuss them at length throughout this volume.

FOCUS ON OBJECTIVES: REQUIRE-MENTS FOR THEIR EFFEC-TIVENESS

Selecting and writing objectives is a crucial activity in the MBO process. We stated earlier that a good objective fills three key functions: (1) to record the commitment of the writer or the organization to achievement of a needed improvement, (2) to provide a measurement of performance, and (3) to motivate the performer. Objectives can accomplish these three purposes best when they are:

written—The process of documenting what is to be done creates a feeling of commitment that a verbal agreement often fails to do. In a complex situation it also is much more reliable than memory. Conversely, beware of the person who scoffs at "writing it down" as so much red tape. This resistance may signal an unwillingness to commit oneself!

supportive—Objectives must complement the overall organizational mission. Sometimes the nature of the support is not obvious immediately—for example, the objectives of the manager of the cafeteria of a downtown bank or government agency. These secondary contributions to the effectiveness of the other operations of the bank or agency are sometimes hard to measure, and become recognized only when discontinued or poorly managed.

important—There are two things to consider here. First, the Pareto principle, stating that 80 percent of effects can be related to 20 percent of the causes. For example, 80 percent of sales volume comes from 20 percent of the customers, and—what is more specifically related to individual objective setting—80 percent of the results produced by a job-holder come as the result of 20 percent of his or her efforts. The important objectives are those associated with maximum results. A second measure of importance is the contribution which the objective promises to one or more of the key results areas of the organization. You will recall that these are the areas in which the organization must concentrate its efforts to ensure long-term success. By definition, neglect of *any* KRA for an extended period will stand in the way of that success. Thus, if the hypothetical organization in Fig. 2 has as its KRAs cost, quality, customer service, safety, and environmental concern, every individual in it must consider objectives which impinge on one or more of these areas. The objective (probably only one of several), selected by the mechanical engineer in that organization obviously is primarily a cost reduction project, but it can also be expected to have a favorable impact on customer service by reducing mandatory downtime on the machines.

interlocking—Your objectives must also complement the efforts of others in lateral positions in the organization. Similarly, you must recruit where needed the efforts of others in complementing your own objectives.

measurable—You must be able to find out when an objective has been achieved. This rule is often distorted to imply that every objective must be expressed in numerical fashion—quantified. *Many objectives cannot be quantified,*[2] but the requirement of *measurability* remains. The measurement may be subjective, based on "feel" or judgment. In turn, feel or judgment is generally based on specific "critical incidents" which indicate that the desired objective has been achieved. An improvement in interpersonal competence of a subordinate may be measured by the absence of unpleasant confrontations with associates, for example. "Completed on schedule" is often a sufficient measurement of attainment of an objective. Such statements, however, should not deter you from seeking more precise quantification wherever possible. "Improved union relations" can be measured by frequency of grievances, proportion of grievances resolved at the verbal level, days lost by work stoppages, etc. "Increased research effectiveness" can be concluded from numbers of patent applications filed, percentage of sales of products developed within the past 2 years, etc. Public relations can be measured by column-inches of favorable or unfavorable "press," by numbers of customer or citizen complaints, and so on. For most fields of endeavor commonly termed "unmeasurable," some kind of measure can be found.

results-oriented—Each objective should be selected for its *contribution* to one or more key results areas, not merely for its *activity* in that area. An objective must *have* an objective—something other than keeping the objective-setter out of mischief. On the other hand, some valid objectives *may* involve an activity which good judgment says will reasonably lead to attainment of the desired goal. For example, if the ultimate objective is to improve interpersonal relations and understanding between a city council and the administrative staff, or between registered nurses and licensed practical nurses in a hospital, an objective to complete a team-building

---

[2]Some MBO authorities have urged that *all* objectives be quantified, or stated in numerical terms. However, preoccupation with "the numbers" can result in the selection of relatively minor objectives that are easily stated as dollar savings, for example, to the neglect of substantial improvement needs which cannot be quantified so easily.

workshop seminar between the two groups by next March is entirely acceptable. If such a meeting is competently developed and conducted by a qualified facilitator, it is a powerful contributor toward the ultimate objective of an improved intergroup working relationship. Even though this objective itself is stated purely in terms of activity and not of results, good judgment identifies it as a worthwhile and potentially productive objective. The key word here is "judgment." Both employee and manager must exercise good judgment to assure that objectives stated in terms of activity are indeed *results-oriented.*

specific and clear—These requirements are so obvious as to need little explanation. Boss and subordinate need to be able to agree at some later date on exactly what was intended. Did the targeted reduction in labor costs include indirect as well as direct labor? What base level of productivity was used in determining the 10 percent reduction—last year's budget or last year's actual? Were the desired results contingent on some specific help or action by the boss? Specificity and clarity prevent confusion over such questions. In addition, they provide greater assurance of achievability than vague, global statements of intent.

time-binding—An objective without a deadline is like a blank check. It provides the subordinate with infinite latitude and requires little commitment. Even a continuing objective toward maintaining a certain level of cost or quality for an indefinite period should include dates as checkpoints for measurement, and for review of opportunities to determine whether the targeted level is still appropriate and how it might be improved.

jointly set and accepted—Mutual development and acceptance of objectives between manager and subordinate provides the primary motivational "plus" in the successful MBO system. The principle here is that people will have a greater commitment to ideas, programs, and decisions which they have helped to create. Such commitment can be expected to result in a higher level of effort and support on the part of the subordinate. Commitment is of course no substitute for the vision and intellectual capacity necessary to *select* the best objectives in the first place, nor for the competence necessary to carry them out. But allowing opportunity for this kind of participation is a way of attracting, keeping, and providing for the continuing growth of competent people, which over a period of time can mean the difference between a good organization and a truly great one. We are speaking here not only of the initial agreement on objectives, but of the process of continual mutual assessment and renegotiation, in a problem-solving environment.

achievable—Achievability means two things. First, it means the difficulty of the job for the individual; it should be difficult enough to provide stretch but not so difficult that frustration is certain to result. (Recall the earlier discussion of the need for establishing two levels of performance.) Second, it means technical feasibility. As stated previously, when we set an objective we should have a plan or alternate methods in mind for achieving it. For example, an objective to improve the productivity of refuse collectors in a city organization (or maintenance mechanics in an airline terminal) by 10 percent by the end of the year is highly suspect unless one or more specific methods or courses of action can be spelled out which give a fighting chance of achieving the 10 percent improvement. When such an objective is desirable, and no feasible plan exists for it, then the formulation of a plan should be made the first-stage objective: "By December 1, evaluate alternatives for the attainment of a 10 percent reduction in indirect labor costs in the warehousing and shipping unit, and present recommended action plan to management for approval."

challenging—There is no surer way of turning MBO into a meaningless paperwork exercise than to use it simply to document what the organization is already doing. This is not only frustrating to the high performers in the organization, but it also ignores the real reasons for adopting MBO: to strive continually for improvement and to increase the responsiveness to change demanded by the environment.

supported by authority—The authority to take necessary action for achieving the objective must be delegated, not only in terms of freedom to take action, but in the assignment of concrete human, financial, and other resources needed to do the job.

backed up by a plan—The plan is an essential part of the objective itself, to verify its achievability, to identify the resources needed to accomplish it, and to provide checkpoints for measuring progress toward it. As we stated above, when no plan exists, the proper first-step objective is to develop one.

The objective-setting process is very important, since the failure of any objective to conform to these standards diminishes its value as an energizer and a directive force for the individual. No matter how thorough and sound the strategic planning, the setting of priorities, the job definition, and all the other prerequisites, the real interface between the individual and the MBO system is the short-term objective. The objective can be a clear and challenging guide to action. It can facilitate productive dialogue between boss and subordinate. It can stimulate personal growth as well as organizational accomplishment. But it can do all these things only in proportion to the care and thought put into it.

WHAT CAN THE ORGANIZATION EXPECT OF MBO?

MBO holds promise for an organization in proportion to the difference between its management system and the one we have described—not as its system appears on paper, but as it actually operates, *and* whether or not it is referred to as "management by objectives." There are exceptions to this rule of thumb. A military or other organization that has traditionally operated with strong direction from the top may actually be thrown off stride—at least temporarily—by the introduction of concepts such as joint objective setting and self-control. All organizations have members who thrive under strongly directive leadership. These individuals may not respond immediately to the humanistic—that is, employee-centered—aspects of MBO.

At the other end of the scale, an organization may be composed of highly creative self-starters, whose output is "discovery" and whose mode is to follow the lead suggested by the most recent experiment in designing the next one. Such people are likely to be turned off by the order, structure, and "mechanization" they see in the MBO approach.

In each of these polar extremes, however, there are potential company benefits from the judicious introduction of the humanistic elements in the first case and the mechanistic or structural improvements in the second. For most organizations the benefits of the MBO system come eventually from both sources. In fact, a management system cannot properly be called MBO unless it does involve both humanistic and structural elements.

The structural elements foster the sense of common direction, the clarity of purpose, the focus on results and standards, and the level of communication and management feedback which the audit and control functions of MBO provide. More specifically, the ultimate benefit derives from:

Effectiveness rather than mere efficiency, "doing the right things" in addition to "doing things right"

More efficient and purposeful communication between levels of management and between employees and their managers

An improved mechanism for rational planning, emphasizing strengths while recognizing weaknesses, the competitive environment, and the needs of the organization's clients or "claimants"

A more rational method for evaluating and rewarding the contributors to success, based on performance rather than on personality traits

A generally more cohesive and informed work force, in which individuals concentrate their efforts on common goals and priorities

The humanistic elements of MBO foster employee autonomy and self-control, participation in the decision-making process, and the feedback which is clearly concerned with the individual's personal development. These are central themes of the mutual objective setting and the performance appraisal and review processes. The benefits appear in the form of a better-performing work force resulting from:

Employees' higher degree of commitment to activities, decisions, and programs which they have played a significant part in creating

Their greater trust of and cooperation with managers because of the helping attitude the latter exhibit toward them

Their realization that rewards depend not only on what gets done, but on how it is accomplished—recognizing the employees' problem-solving and coping behavior, and in general treating them as unique individuals

The interest shown in their personal growth and development

The *immediate* potential for your organization may lie in either one or both of these areas. The organization which is in disarray may well concentrate its effort first on restructuring, and may institute the humanistic emphasis at a later point. We note such an evolution especially in the performance appraisal system. The pre-MBO system is more than likely a checklist of personality traits (cooperativeness, attitude, initiative, etc.). The structural emphasis of MBO puts appraisal on much firmer ground: performance. The humanistic emphasis puts back into the equation a personality dimension, as noted above, but one which must not overlook the measures of objective performance.

To summarize, taking a polar position on the "true" meaning and purpose of MBO can result in failure to utilize its full potential. An organization may profitably introduce the system in either way, mechanistic or humanistic, depending on the present status of its management system—but always with an eye to the future benefits of going all the way.

WHAT MBO IS NOT: SOME MIS-CONCEPTIONS

Through the years a number of misconceptions have arisen to becloud the MBO issue. They point up the widespread superficiality of understanding to which we referred earlier. Aggravated by overenthusiastic claims by MBO's promoters, and by the horror stories related by those who attempted to apply it without sufficient preparation, these misconceptions have created a negative climate in many organizations, preventing a rational discussion of MBO as a potential improvement in management practice. We conclude this brief overview of MBO with a list of prevalent claims and statements to which we add a few words of refutation or clarification.

"Another new gimmick, soon forgotten . . ."

By now we hope you understand that MBO is not a gimmick, but rather a system of total management. Furthermore, it is not new. It is an articulation of management functions and processes that characterize the work of the better managers in the most effective organizations. First defined and described in the 1950s, it is not likely to die out or be forgotten as long as there is a need for creative managers dedicated to organizational improvement.

"A highly complex and theoretical concept developed in the ivory tower by academicians"

True, the concepts were first articulated in the universities, but by management authorities with a decidedly real-world orientation. These researchers and consultants made a real contribution by documenting and systematizing the very practical methods developed by their clients.

"Purports to be an 'easy out' for managers . . ."

This could not be further from the truth. MBO is a most demanding system of management. There is, as far as we know, no easy road to effective management over the long term. Some proponents have described the system as simply an informal, periodic, verbal, or "back of an envelope" contract between a manager and an employee, promising vast results. The contract is indeed a part of MBO, but the results depend on a great deal more than that.

"A panacea for all organizational ills . . ."

Insofar as good management practices can identify and ultimately solve many problems in the organization, MBO can qualify as a "broad spectrum" antidote. But it is no cure for incompetence, and no insurance against such forces as inflation, foreign competition, and government intervention. Its practice will build competence, but it also *requires* competence. And it can help the organization adapt to, if not foresee and avoid the impact of, the uncontrollable factors.

"A typical 'campaign': a big flurry and it's all over . . ."

Unfortunately, this is the form the implementation takes in many organizations. The initial effort is to produce a set of objectives. All levels of management set to work, the big book is published, and the whole organization lapses into a state of normalcy until the next campaign. But such an approach, as we have seen, does not produce an MBO system.

"Only for large production organizations, where output can be 'counted'"

Operations whose output can be counted tend to have an easier time of setting objectives, but they benefit most from the objectives they set in the intangible areas. Organizations large or small, whose output is all intangible—a school guidance office, for instance—need MBO even more than the production operation.

"A 'paper mill' that bogs you down in a morass of forms and reports . . ."

This is probably the most legitimate of all the critical comments on our list. Documentation *can* become a major problem. However, it can be kept under control. We will suggest some ways to avoid paperwork problems later on.

"A punitive approach to managing people . . ."

This belief comes from early attempts to simplify performance appraisal by measuring only how fully an employee met the stated objectives. Since the employee was supposed to set the objective in the first place, MBO quickly got the reputation of "giving them enough rope to hang themselves." Needless to say, this feeling on the part of employees was something more than paranoia. This is still one of the most frequently encountered stumbling blocks in the way of implementing MBO. If these kinds of employee attitudes have been instilled by past management practices, managers must be very sensitive in handling the joint objective setting process and in performance appraisal. At best it will take time and patience, through several cycles of appraisal and feedback, to get the point across that managers are there to help the employee be successful.

The other units of this volume deal with the performance appraisal and employee development processes. Before turning to the next unit, however, work through the exercises for this unit. The first one will give you an opportunity to assess your job and your organization, as they are and as they might be affected by an MBO system of the type we have described. The second is a test of your understanding of the process.

Most of the units in this entire series are followed by one or more exercises. Try to complete each unit's exercises before reading on. You will get much more insight into the MBO process if you do the exercises.

We will offer a few words of comment or interpretation following each exercise. This is to give you feedback on your performance wherever possible. In relatively few instances do we provide answers, because the proportion of cases or problems where anyone other than you can *know* the answer is small. Most exercises (like the two in this unit) involve analysis of your own job situation or organization, or they present situations into which *you* must project *yourself.* Our commentary, therefore, is often in the form of suggestions—about facets of the problem which are typically overlooked, or about further work you can do on your own to apply the principles and methods of MBO on the job.

You will find the exercises demanding of your thought, time, and energy. Do them thoughtfully and carefully. You will get much more out of the books if you complete *every* exercise, because the exercises address important points not covered in the text. You will understand better many of the difficulties that may arise in applying MBO principles by *first* exposing yourself to the problems in the exercises and *then* reading about their possible solutions.

Finally, remember what we said in the beginning, that MBO requires a great deal of commitment. How you respond to these exercises is a test of your commitment, and probably a good predictor of your success in tackling MBO.

26

EXERCISE 1A   1.   List the critically important duties, responsibilities, and results which your job should, under ideal conditions, contribute to the organization.

2.   List any other duties which interfere with your fulfilling the critical obligations listed above.

3. List any problems (organizational, procedural, policy, interpersonal, etc.) which prevent you from contributing to the organization as effectively as you wish.

4. Select the most critical interferences and problems you have identified. Referring to the MBO definition and flow process diagram (Fig. 1), in which aspect or element of MBO might you expect to find an answer or solution? Describe the possible actions you might take and the results you might expect from them.

EXERCISE 1B We haven't truly learned a concept until we can explain it to others. Listed below are several questions which have come up in introductory seminars, from managers hearing about MBO for the first time. Test your understanding of the overall process as we have presented it in Unit 1 by responding to these neophytes. Fill in the key points of your response on the next page. Practice giving the full response verbally to an associate or to a mirror.

1. "Why this laborious process of looking at major responsibilities or KRAs; thinking up 'ultimate levels of performance' and *then* setting objectives? I know what my job is; it's to cut costs. Why not just let me set objectives—period?"

2. "It sounds like MBO just consists of writing down what I'm already doing. This is only taking my time away from doing it, and then holding my feet to the fire because I don't bat a thousand."

3. "A formal performance appraisal will do nothing but inflame my people! We don't have a merit pay system in our city. How can I motivate a person by giving her an excellent review and then not reward her with extra pay?"

4. "Suppose my manager asks my unit to contribute a share of our division's overall cost reduction target. Wouldn't I be a fool to commit myself to a figure unless I already had action plans to tell me how I'd reach that figure?"

5. "How can I be sure an employee isn't 'snowing' me with an easy objective by claiming that's all he can possibly do?"

6. "This idea of 'joint' objective setting is ridiculous. My boss passes some of them down to me from on high, and I propose some of my own to him. What's 'joint' about that? Doesn't it just mean that I accept his and then whatever time is left I use to work on my own?"

Statement   **Key Points in Response**

1.

2.

3.

4.

5.

6.

Commentary on Exercise 1A

We suggest that you first review your entries in questions 1, 2, and 3 for clarity and specificity. If, for example, in part 3 you have tended to use one- or two-word entries such as "communication," "restrictive policy," and "uncooperative coworkers," go back and give it more thought. Identifying workable solutions is difficult if the problem is not well defined. Once the problem areas are defined, however, you should find answers to many of them in the MBO process.

You may also have been tempted to look for solutions in the MBO system that are not there. MBO is not the answer to all the problems an organization can accumulate. It will not create competent managers or technicians out of incompetent ones (though it will help identify the areas where competence is lacking). Neither will it take you out of a business you should not be in (though it may force you to answer the question of why you are in it). Keep your expectations at a reasonable level and apply MBO to systemic problems of planning, communication, control, and growth. Over time it will even help eliminate basic problems that may appear to be insoluble.

This exercise and others that focus on your own situation lend themselves to group thinking and consensus seeking as well as to individual study. The *Leader's Manual* which accompanies the series is designed to help you work with others in group sessions designed to introduce an MBO system into your organization.

Commentary on Exercise 1B

Your replies to these questions might have included the following points:

1. The simple answer is that knowing where you're going helps in taking the first step. However, concentrating on the short-range objective entails two additional risks. First, by jumping too quickly to a short-term objective you may be foreclosing the opportunity to do what the authorities on creativity call "divergent thinking," that is, thinking about a problem area (or key results area) broadly and thereby keeping your options open. Converging too quickly on a specific solution tends to close the gate on other, possibly better ideas, keeping them locked up in your subconscious. It also puts you in the position of coming up with a solution before you fully understand the problem. In this case, the problem which your

organization is facing may require a greater contribution from you in an area other than cost—for example, in quality or customer service. Covering all the KRAs helps ensure that your cost-oriented efforts won't hurt results in quality, safety, labor relations, or some other KRA perhaps even more important. (What *are* your KRAs?)

2. If objectives are truly just a statement of what you are already doing, you have missed the whole *objective* of managing by objectives — namely the improvement of individual and organizational effectiveness. Let's rethink your objectives. Start with KRAs and look at long-range goals. What is your job going to require of you in 5 or 10 years? You'd better start planning to get there *now.*

    If you feel that your boss is out to trap you, then your problem is more serious than your doubts about MBO — it's a problem of mistrust, and you should try to get to the bottom of it, whether or not you are operating in an MBO system.

3. Of course, you know your people better than anyone else — or do you? People *do* stay on their jobs for reasons other than pay. If your pay plan is being administered equitably, and if jobs are classified and priced so that your people can understand the structure, they should be able to accept the facts of life. (Have you *communicated* the pay plan to them?) Anyhow, it's a mistake to think that the appraisal itself is the motivator. The *real* motivation came from the opportunity to do that superior piece of work and from the achievement itself. A good peformance review is merely good, positive recognition, which can help keep that motivation alive. It also affirms your interest in your employee's future growth. This interest may help *keep the employee around,* so that you'll have a good candidate when the next opportunity for a promotion or an upgrade comes along. To fail in giving positive recognition to your better performers either risks losing them from the organization entirely or encourages them to perform at the lowest common denominator. With really good employees, it's usually the former that happens.

4. This is a "chicken or egg" question. Which comes first, the objective or the plan of action? In fact, the two are inseparable, and you really can't say that you have firmly established an objective until you have examined the courses of action open to you for achieving it. The process is one of matching needs and potential contributions, and there is no guarantee that the match will be perfect the first time around. It's somewhat easier to do when you are the initiator yourself and have an innovative proposal to reduce cost, for example. In this case your cost objective becomes your own evaluation of what the results of your efforts will be. But when responding to a

higher level need, it's best to give an honest estimate of what your contribution will be. If a gap exists, set an objective of identifying ways to close it.

5. At the functional level in an organization, there is no substitute for a manager's knowledge of the workers and of the technology involved in the function for which the manager is responsible. If you are new to the organization, you will of course have to rely more heavily on your technical knowledge at first. The question, however, seems to overlook the fact that MBO requires a continually dynamic management style in which manager and subordinate continue to learn about each other. The observant, energetic manager will soon spot the performer whose tendency is to hold back. MBO cannot substitute for intelligence and effort on the part of managers.

6. Some organizational needs are nonnegotiable "musts." (The corporate profit improvement target in Fig. 2 is a typical one.) Joint objective setting, however, refers to more than the fact that the objectives which an individual sets are partly "imposed" by others and partly "volunteered" by the individual. It refers also to the facts that the boss assumes responsibility for helping to remove obstacles in the way of the employee, that there is mutual agreement on the priorities of the individual's objectives, that there is agreement on personal development objectives for the employee, and that very often the boss as well as the subordinate may have to "give" a little, especially on the exact method to be used in reaching the objective. Joint objective setting also means coming to an agreement on what went wrong and what went right when the objective is reviewed, and having a mutual willingness to revise, tighten up, drop, or otherwise modify the objective based on the review.

UNIT 2

PERFORMANCE APPRAISAL
A PROCESS AND A RELATIONSHIP

The history of performance appraisal is a long and unhappy one. Scarcely a year goes by without one or more major articles in management literature restating its potential for improving organizational and individual performance, but bemoaning the fact that this potential remains largely untapped. Sometimes the culprit in the scenario is the manager who has failed to realize the critical importance of this activity. Or else, it is the outmoded system of appraisal currently in use. Sometimes it is MBO itself, for an alleged mechanistic approach that tends to ignore the human elements and sees only *what* was accomplished, not *how* it was done or what problems were faced or overcome in the process.

In this volume, we will give you an opportunity to analyze your own performance appraisal system or procedure and transform it into one that naturally evolves from the principles of MBO, embodying both the structural (or "mechanistic" as the critics would have it) and the humanistic benefits. As we noted in Unit 1, the performance appraisal process consists of (1) the day-by-day assessment of progress, (2) the continual problem solving that keeps things moving, (3) periodic progress reviews wherein the manager and the employee assess results and replan future efforts if necessary, and (4) an infrequent but regular appraisal of the employee's performance and potential. This performance appraisal process concerns itself with both the *what* and the *how* of the employee's performance and considers to the greatest extent possible the needs of the employee as well as those of the organization.

Today almost every manager subscribes to the premise that an organization must concern itself with the needs of its employees. The performance appraisal process is a tool admirably suited to satisfying employees' needs for help, recognition, and personal growth. In practice, however, most appraisal systems fulfill few if any of these essential purposes. They vary, in the view of many managers, from a mere formality designed vaguely

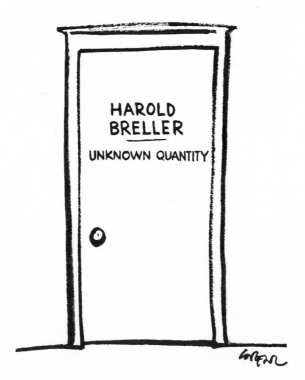

to justify an annual salary adjustment to a punitive—and usually futile—attempt to improve marginal performance.

One problem is that the relationship of boss and subordinate itself gives rise to differences in perception of what the "real" needs of the employee are, and to feelings that get in the way of a productive problem-solving dialogue. All too often, both boss and subordinate adopt a defensive position (often manifested as an *aggressive* posture), which reduces the appraisal to a meaningless exercise that avoids the whole issue of performance improvement. If the employee's performance is marginal and the issue *cannot* be avoided, the appraisal turns into an unpleasant confrontation.

It is of course unrealistic to suppose that the needs of the organization and those of the employee can always be congruent. Some conflict will inevitably be present. The organization may not be able to provide added responsibilities as fast as a bright, young employee can absorb them. Nor can jobs always be designed to eliminate the routine drudgery that frustrates the professional. Unfortunately, problems like these often are ignored or neglected. A deterioration in performance may result unless the problems are acknowledged by both parties and plans made to circumvent or alleviate them.

The MBO system provides a framework in which performance is measured against agreed-on objectives selected to give support to the overall mission and strategy of the organization. This framework is, however, only the beginning of the appraisal process. Measuring employees' performance cannot by itself satisfy their psychological needs. Neither can it induce employees to change their behavior in the direction of *improved* performance. It is at this point that the structural features of MBO reach the limit of their usefulness and it becomes necessary to rely on the more humanistic principles associated with interpersonal feedback and joint objective setting. Without these principles, MBO can degenerate into a mechanistic system consisting mostly of volumes of procedures and plans that occupy shelf space and produce little benefit to the organization. Joint objective setting can be a real benefit even to a well-managed organization that is functioning at a high level of technical competence, and with a well-understood and accepted sense of direction.

There are several reasons for the rule that objectives should normally be established in a participative mode: (1) from a pragmatic standpoint, much more realistic objectives will be set if the person who knows the most about the job gets involved; (2) people are more committed to—and motivated by—objectives that they have helped create; and (3) the *manager* also is committed to helping achieve the objective. This process is further discussed in Unit 7 of this volume and at much greater length in Vol. II.

Still, even when objectives are set in this manner, they often become "cast in concrete" and serve more to misguide than to keep the organization or the individual on course. Frequent review can prevent your objectives from losing their directive power in this way. In addition to providing for the satisfaction of employees' needs and guiding and motivating them to higher levels of performance, the performance appraisal process serves to keep MBO a living system rather than a dusty monument.

The key to both of these advantages is a closer, more understanding relationship between boss and subordinate on a one-to-one, face-to-face basis. This relationship includes not only the typical periodic (usually annual) formal review sessions, but also the day-to-day contacts that involve exchange of information and discussion of problems and progress.

To get a baseline measurement of both your own performance and the appraisal system in your organization, complete Exercises 2A and 2B.

EXERCISE 2A   Describe, in the space below, the most recent performance appraisal you received from your immediate superior. Consider the following questions, then write your comments in the space provided.

1. How much help was offered by your boss? Asked for by you? To what extent did this affect your feelings of independence, self-control, or satisfaction with the appraisal process?

2. How much did you learn about yourself and your work during the session? What, specifically, did you learn? How much did your boss learn about you and your work?

3. To what extent were plans made for your future development or growth? Describe briefly.

4. Did the session deal with planning and objective setting for the next appraisal period? To what extent?

5. If job problems were discussed, how effective was the session in finding solutions?

6. Overall, what effect has the session had on your subsequent work performance?

EXERCISE 2B Check the appropriate column for both "Frequency" and "Effect on my Performance" for each of the following events as they occur between you and your boss.

	Frequency				Effect on my Performance				
	Frequent	Occasional	Seldom	Rare	Highly Favorable	Favorable	Neutral	Negative	Highly Negative
Contacts initiated by me to discuss my progress and the problems I am having on the job									
Contacts initiated by my boss to discuss my progress and the problems I am having on the job									
Unsolicited favorable comments to me by my boss about my work									
Unsolicited unfavorable comments to me by my boss about my work									
Information shared with me by my boss that provides me with new facts or background needed to do my job									
Help solicited for me by my boss from others who have information or resources that I need to do my job									
New projects or objectives given me by my boss between formal objective-setting sessions									
Information shared by me with my boss to alert him or her to problems not related to my own job									
Questions addressed to me by my boss seeking more information about my written reports and recommendations									

Commentary on Exercise 2A

If your answer to question 6 reveals that the session had little lasting effect on your work performance, you are probably among the majority of employees. Temporary negative effects on performance are frequently encountered after a critical appraisal session; if you were rewarded with a substantial pay increase, this may have had an equally transitory euphoria effect.

Longer-lasting effects, however, are likely to be the result of the planning and objective setting done during the appraisal discussions, and the help offered by the manager in removing roadblocks from your path and providing personal insights and development opportunities. If your answers to questions 1 to 5 reflect this type of result, you have a boss who is skilled in the kind of appraisal we advocate. You should try to emulate his or her example in dealing with your subordinates. In any case, we suggest that you repeat this exercise based on your last appraisal session with one of your own subordinates. You will have to make the appropriate changes in the pronouns in questions 1 to 3, and of course you may have to infer your employee's feelings. When finished, compare your practices with those of your boss. This may give you some leads on how to improve your own performance, or on how to work with your boss so that both of you can improve your skills.

Several supplementary comments may be of help to you. The "helper" role (question 1) is an extremely important one in this appraisal system (and in management in general), but it can be overdone. If you felt resentful during or after your session with your boss over his or her interference, or came away feeling inadequate, of if the "help" appeared to reflect lack of trust in you or unwillingness to delegate, the help was probably misdirected or overdone. Avoid this trap in your own appraisals.

In question 2 you were asked how much you learned. You should expect an effective manager to have a broader perspective on the overall situation and to know some things about your job in that context that you may not. However, if the appraisal process is working properly, you should *not* be surprised by being told that your activities were not in support of the objectives as the boss sees them, or by the boss giving you negative feedback on things that happened a long time ago and that you never before realized were important.

This latter problem may reflect excessive reliance on the periodic formal review session and neglect of the equally important day-to-day dialogue, which is the other side of the appraisal process.

Commentary on Exercise 2B

The more checks you placed in the "frequent" and "occasional" columns, the more productively the day-to-day opportunities for appraisal are being used by you and your boss. This applies even to unfavorable comments about your performance, although in most situations we would expect these to be occasional rather than frequent and to be balanced by an equal or greater frequency of positive comments. Likewise, a certain number of "new" objectives, unplanned activities, and revised priorities are likely to result on any job, and you must be able to cope with them. Too many such events, however, may be symptomatic of insufficient planning, a fuzzy organizational mission, or a sloppy job description. An overcommitment to new objectives in a job situation that is strongly response-oriented, or in which a readiness-to-serve posture must be maintained, may also result in many frustrating changes in priorities.

Your ratings of the effectiveness of the daily appraisal tools listed in the exercise are of course a function of how your boss makes or responds to the various types of contact. However, the ratings may also tell you something about yourself. Are you over-sensitive to criticism? Do frequent changes or new demands throw you off-balance? Do you resent questions about your written reports, which you view as superb examples of clarity and conciseness? Are you writing for yourself instead of for the reader?

You may have wondered why contacts initiated and information volunteered by you belong in the category of informal appraisal of your performance. They are there because *self*-appraisal is the most efficient type of measurement, and an awareness of when you have reached the limits of your capabilities must therefore enter the picture. These contacts also provide your boss with inputs that will help him or her determine your development needs; they will also help in revising objectives for others as well as for yourself. Naturally it is difficult for a subordinate to discuss inadequacies and development needs with the boss, unless there is a high degree of trust between the two persons. One of the purposes of this volume is to help you develop that trust.

You may feel uncomfortable about responding to questions about how your boss does things. We are asking you to do this because you need to know to what extent your own practices are a reflection of your leader's, and also because all but a very few managers in an organization have the dual role of boss and subordinate. We are therefore asking you to put yourself in both pairs of shoes. As you did in Exercise 1A, repeat Exercise 1B rating your own use of these appraisal tools in dealing with a particular subordinate or, if you wish, with each subordinate. The latter approach may provide insights on the different styles you use with different subordinates. You will have to infer the "effect on my performance" feelings of your subordinates if you do not have sufficient evidence of these.

Finally, examine the items you have checked as "negative" or "highly negative" in their effect on performance, and determine whether it is a matter of overuse, underuse, or misuse. Then ask yourself "Why?" Lack of skill? Lack of time? Lack of awareness of the importance of the tool? If lack of time to do the job right appears to be the problem, read or review Vol. II. If lack of awareness or skill is the problem, take heart—we'll work on these as you continue through this book.

UNIT 3

THE EVOLUTION OF RESULTS-BASED APPRAISAL

THE PURPOSES OF APPRAISAL

By completing the exercises that follow the last unit, you obtained a feel for the purposes and methods of the results-oriented appraisal process which is necessary to make an MBO system work. A primary purpose is to "close the loop," using feedback from the appraisal process to reestablish and refine the work objectives to ensure that they achieve the desired improvement in performance. The day-to-day contacts between manager and subordinate provide the early-warning system needed to prevent drift. The periodic appraisal and progress review discussions provide the longer-range perspective on how the job is going and what needs to be done.

In this and the following units we will emphasize the motivational power of the relationship between boss and subordinate to produce better results for the organization and help the employee find greater job satisfaction and personal growth. To these ends, the appraisal process provides a rational basis for determining

43

compensation and other forms of recognition and reward for the top performer and a chance to achieve for those who are turned on by the thrill of accomplishment. It also leads to a generally greater concern for the personal and professional growth of all employees. At the same time, the benefits to the manager and the organization are substantial. Promotion decisions can be made more rationally, and the often unpleasant decision to transfer or terminate an unsatisfactory employee can become easier, because it is made with more confidence in the validity and the humanity of the decision process—there will be ample documented evidence of attempts along the way to salvage the person. And, of course, the organization benefits from the greater interest, effort, and concern generated in its employees.

The impetus to improve performance provided by the feedback process can be explained by motivational theory. We will not go into all the theories of motivation, but will merely state a few principles to help you understand the effects of feedback on human behavior.

In one view of human motivation, all behavior is in response to one or more internal driving forces termed *needs.* Although people are often unaware of the presence of a specific psychological need, it can be inferred by their response to any of a group of related *goal objects.* These goal objects are thought to provide relief from the tension caused by a specific need, and are in themselves valued by the individual. The need acts as both an *energizer* and a *directive force*—directive because relief is obtained by behavior directed toward certain specific goal objects or organizational inducements. It is believed that several needs can be satisfied by a good appraisal/feedback system. They include:

> *n-achievement*—The favorable response of a person to opportunities for reaching moderately difficult goals or objectives for which the person has aptitude (and a reasonable chance of success) is thought to indicate the presence of a *need for achievement,* (n-achievement).[1] And persons who exhibit those responses to

---

[1] n-achievement has been extensively studied by David C. McClelland and is covered in his book *The Achieving Society,* (Princeton: Van Nostrand, 1961). McClelland finds it characteristic of certain cultures, and associates its presence with the economic and social advancement of whole societies.

challenging objectives are called *achievers,* i.e., they are high in n-achievement. Achievers are motivated, according to this theory, by the design of jobs and the work environment to provide moderately challenging work and facilitate its completion. The achiever will respond, and his or her accomplishment is the goal object that satisfies the need.

While the initial objective-setting process does not in itself provide the motivation, it is obvious that success in reaching those objectives, aided by the availability of help from the manager when needed, acts as a valued goal object, and can stimulate the achieving person to continued effort. Participation in the objective-setting process adds commitment, and the manger's positive feedback in the appraisal sessions acts to affirm the success in the mind of the individual. Repeated failures on the job can be very upsetting to high achievers, perhaps forcing them to seek other goal objects (which may be off the job). It is especially important that the manager allow maximum freedom to high achievers in setting objectives. The achiever will generally set goals that provide enough stimulus for improvement without a great deal of input from the boss.

n-predictability—This is a need for some degree of assurance that measurements will be consistent and that, for example, management will not continually be changing its collective mind about what the job is, where the organization is going, etc. The satisfiers or goal objects are: (1) documented and reasonably stable plans, (2) managers who appraise on the basis of agreed-upon objectives rather than shifting standards, and (3) managers who do not hide things from their employees, especially standards of performance.

n-equity—This is a need to feel that one is being treated in relation to one's contribution, and especially in relation to the contributions of others. The appraisal process can satisfy this need in obvious ways.

The last two needs give rise to tensions which, if not relieved, are definitely *de*motivating in their effect. When these needs are satisfied they do not generally provide a strong positive motivation, but when frustrated they can have adverse effects on morale and, if the frustration is prolonged or severe enough, it can result in the loss of good people from the organization. Psychologist Frederick Herzberg has found that when the individual senses problems with the organization that, in effect remove the goal objects necessary to fulfill these kinds of needs, the result is negative motivation. On the other hand, satisfying the higher-level needs for achievement, recognition, and self-actualization (the urge to be the best that one can possibly become) provides positive motivation.[2] We feel that frustration of these higher-level needs can also be demotivating, like frustration of the equity and predictability needs. In any case, whether by removing demotivating forces or augmenting motivating ones, it is clear that positive feedback can aid the organization and the individual in the search for greater effectiveness. This presupposes an organizational structuring that assures pay plans that are equitable and consistently applied from component to component, managers whose behavior is predictable, and job designs that can provide opportunities for achievers.

These are some of the reasons for the development of a results-oriented appraisal system—one that builds on a sound structural foundation and provides the goal objects we have mentioned.

FEEDBACK FOR WHOM? Performance appraisal systems that preceded MBO had one common fault (and still have it, because they are far more in evidence than the results-oriented system)—they provided information which was helpful to management while offering the employees little that was of use in improving or correcting their performance.[3] It is even doubtful whether these systems were really useful to management for making decisions about salary increases, or for identifying personnel to be promoted or terminated "if the recession deepens"—decisions which in fact could probably be made almost as accurately by a feel for the situation. As an example, managers in industry and government have on occasion been asked to identify (and, less frequently, to give the bad news to) the "bottom 5 percent" of their personnel. In this decision, which

---

[2]Frederick Herzberg, *Work and the Nature of Man* (Cleveland: World, 1966), pp. 75-77.

[3]Feedback occurs on two different levels. First there is the feedback we described in our discussion of the MBO cycle in Unit 1—the kind the organization uses to tell how it is doing—and, second, feedback to the *individual* to answer the question "How am *I* doing?" We are now talking about the second kind.

should be a real test of the appraisal system, that system is often ignored and the classification made by judgment alone.

The deficiency common to most old-line appraisal systems was that they attempted to describe not the individual's performance but the individual himself, mostly in terms so general that they were meaningless. The original basis was a series of traits and habits such as "cooperativeness," "positive attitude," "dependability," "initiative," and other traits that were equally important but subject to a great deal of interpretation. A few other characteristics were included, such as "quantity and quality of work," and "punctuality," to which objective measurements could have been applied. Even here, however, the common practice was to rate people on each of these attributes on a scale of 0 to 5 or 0 to 10, with a few canned guidelines to help the manager decide where to place the checkmarks on the scale. Here is an example of a scale with such standardized comments:

		Cooperation			
unacceptable					excellent
0	1	2	3	4	5
Unable to work with others		Few clashes: usually willing to do teamwork	Always a good team-worker		Goes out of his way to be helpful, a real team-player

The conscientious manager, baffled by such "helpful" comments, was usually forced to resort to judgment. Since this was the case, it was difficult to justify the ratings to the employee, and in many cases no attempt was made even to communicate the manager's verdict to the person being rated. Often this made little difference, however, since either there was no merit pay plan in effect, or, when there *was* latitude for differential raises, the manager again resorted to judgment.

The latter decision — how to slice the salary-increase pie — was sometimes aided by a *forced ranking* of all employees by the manager. Employees were ranked on each of the attributes, a point score assigned for each rank, and the point scores for each employee totaled over all of the attributes. The relative scores provided some guidance in determining who received how much of an increase.

Since the comments on the scales led to rigidity and failed to give adequate guidance, an obvious modification evolved — a blank space adjacent to each scale for comments supporting the manager's evaluation. However, many managers still used open-ended comments which strongly resembled the original canned phrases, and, after a time, the *critical-incident* approach emerged. This approach, which embodies the principles of MBO and retains its usefulness in our current results-oriented appraisal system, simply requests a description of specific behavior on the job that reflects the presence or absence of the attribute being measured. As it has been practiced, however, it has been used by the manager primarily to make more rational decisions in the rating, ranking, and rewarding processes rather than to give direct feedback to the employee. In fact, many employees, aware of its use but not privy to the results, refer to it as the "little black book" method.

The advent of MBO in the early 1950s, with its primary focus on structure and output, provided firm directions on what should be measured. Concurrently, MBO's emphasis on the behavioral sciences stressed the importance of the methods of measurement, particularly self-measurement, to the individual. The two emphases are complementary and both play a vital role in the MBO approach to performance appraisal. This approach retains a great deal that is good from the more traditional practices we have just described. You may still be using one of these methods in your organization. If so, don't throw out the baby with the bath water when you decide to adopt the MBO process of appraisal. Retain or modify those elements that are achieving the purposes we have laid out. You will have a chance to examine your present practices as you proceed to do Exercise 3.

In the next unit we will discuss how and to what extent a manager can provide feedback on the important but difficult-to-measure personality traits and attributes.

EXERCISE 3 1. Arm yourself with your organization's current performance appraisal policy or procedure and whatever forms are used in its implementation.

2. Observe, or find out by discussing with other managers, how it is being implemented.

3. Comment on how well the various purposes of an appraisal process (as discussed in Unit 3) are being achieved by your procedure. Suggest improvements.

Purpose	**Rating and Comments**
"Closing the loop" — for review and readjustment of objectives	
"On the spot" control of deviations	
Positive stimulus to individual performance	

Purpose

Information to management
for decision on salary

Rating and Comments

Information to management
for promotion decisions

Assistance to employee on
career or personal de-
velopment

Commentary on Exercise 3

We hope you didn't simply use the generality "Adopt MBO system" as your suggestion for improvement in every case in which you felt your system was not achieving its purpose. What we are looking for are *specific* ways to ensure more purposeful appraisal. Furthermore, it may not be in the cards (at least not in the hand you are holding now) to scrap your present system. It may not even be desirable—the more you can retain your present procedures or modify them to include MBO principles, the easier it will be to implement MBO in your organization.

Some parts of your organization may not even become involved in MBO at all. Highly programmed, repetitive jobs with little or no opportunity for individual development or initiative are not easily adaptable. How about your hourly work force? Are they appraised? How would you modify *their* system?

Your suggestions might include such nonrevolutionary changes as (1) doing more frequent appraisals, (2) discussing them with the employee, (3) reviewing the list of traits being rated and making comments as to how each trait is affecting the employee's performance, (4) using more critical incidents in rating (and ensuring that the incidents are performance-related), and (5) setting at least one improvement target for each employee in some critical area of the job.

There is much that can be done to improve the usefulness of even the most formal and perfunctory annual appraisal routine. Don't let it remain a routine!

UNIT 4

PERSONALITY AND THE APPRAISAL PROCESS

Early proponents of the MBO appraisal system, in a sharp pendulum swing away from a trait-oriented appraisal, tended to put too much stress on the appraisal of *what* was accomplished to the almost complete exclusion of *how* it was accomplished. At least this was the impression received by many behavior-oriented management theorists, who quickly adopted the position that MBO was just a mechanistic system that contained none of the precious human elements. This of course was a misunderstanding, since there was no attempt on the part of the MBO theorists to eliminate consideration of how a job was accomplished; they were merely trying to deemphasize the hitherto completely trait-oriented approach.

Obviously, for any task, the way in which it is accomplished must be judged as well as the degree of achievement. For example, a person who achieves an objective by figuratively walking over the backs of associates to get there has not done the most productive job for the organization. If the achiever has commandeered more than his or her share of the available resources, and in the process has deprived others of resources needed to get their jobs done, it is conceivable that the accomplishment of the job may have *cost* the organization overall, rather than helping it achieve its objective. Similarly, a salesman who achieves his sales bogie by making promises which the manufacturing division finds it impossible to keep may irreparably damage the reputation of the company.

We could cite endless examples of how failure to evaluate how a job was done would be unfair either to the organization or to the individual. As an example of unfairness to the individual, consider the case of an employee who strives to achieve a very difficult objective and is able to reach only what we will call an 85 percent achievement level. It is quite conceivable that the effort and ingenuity required to achieve that level may warrant a more favorable appraisal than the effort and ingenuity of an employee who achieved 100 percent on an easier objective. It is difficult for us to conceive, therefore, of any objective appraisal of an employee's performance that does not include the how as well as the what.

THE EFFECT OF PERSONALITY ON THE OR-GANIZATION

The insistence that performance be appraised solely on the basis of what was accomplished rather than taking account of the personality of the employee still retains some currency. ''Appraise the work and not the individual'' remains one of the most frequently quoted principles.

Nevertheless, there are sound reasons for discussing personality in appraisal sessions, even though it may seem like an invasion of privacy for a manager to stress these matters with an employee. The fact is that the *personality of an individual is nothing more than the sum total of his or her characteristic reactions or responses to the environment. It reflects the individual's adjustment to his or her surroundings.* Personality can also be defined as the internal organization of an individual's needs, motives, thought patterns, and habits, which determine those characteristic responses. It is therefore the ruling factor in determining how a person goes about getting the job done. To put it another way, if how a task is accomplished is important to the appraisal process then so is personality.

Personality represents the totality of unique behavioral responses that distinguishes one person from another. Differences in personality dictate that while one employee will tackle a problem aggressively, head-on, another will look for alternatives to circumvent the problem. Often the results are equally good. In such cases, it would be unwise for the manager to impose the same approach on both employees, or, in other words, to attempt to change the personality of one or the other. Sometimes, however, the "problems" the individual is tackling are other *people.* In this case, personality can be a strong factor, either positive or negative. Earlier in this unit we gave examples of such effects, commenting on the potential damage to the organization as a whole, in the form of ill will from other employees in the first case, and from an important customer in the second. Personality should certainly enter the discussion between manager and employee whenever the organization is affected in this way.

OTHER PERSONALITY EFFECTS
We are generally our own worst enemies. Individual personality problems affect the organization in varying degrees, depending upon the position of the individual and the degree to which his or her actions affect other employees, customers, stock market analysts, union officials, suppliers, bankers, and others who contribute effort or resources to the organization. But the effects *on the individual* can obviously be much greater. The way in which an individual comes across to others can either help or hinder the achievement of his or her work objectives. Even when there is no harmful effect on performance in one's present position, the way one tackles human or technical problems can be a major factor in determining career progress, especially when one is being considered as a future manager.

Personality is therefore a topic of tremendous interest to the individual as well as to the organization. If you are reluctant to discuss these things with your employees because of concern about invasion of privacy or for other reasons, ask yourself whether your reluctance is really in his or her best interests, or in your own, especially if poor performance is keeping your unit from achieving its goals.

A little reflection will indicate that these are matters which should and must be discussed. The question is "how?"

TRAITS AND CRITICAL INCIDENTS

We most certainly do not recommend a return to the trait-rating system of performance appraisal. However, we must somehow bring personality traits into the appraisal process, and the medium we will use is the *critical incident.* This is simply an observed or reliably reported example of the use of the trait in the work situation that significantly affected the person's performance. (A frequent occurence of a seemingly insignificant behavior can also become significant. Such a chain of events also fits our description.) Critical incidents can also offer good or bad examples of performance itself but for the present we will concentrate on incidents that demonstrate the positive or negative use of a personality trait.

There are dangers here, both in accumulating the information and in communicating it to the employee. They lie in the fact that many traits are given more than one name, depending on whether they are used to a degree that is appropriate to the situation, excessively, or insufficiently. Since the appropriate degree is a matter of judgment, one rater might decide that an incident indicates forthrightness, while another might categorize the same incident as tactless. Other pairs of adjectives or descriptive phrases that different raters might use to categorize identical incidents are:

forceful	aggressive
cooperative	compliant
methodical	plodding
self-confident	egotistical
takes initiative	opportunistic
visionary	impractical
decisive	autocratic
strong convictions	opinionated
firm	stubborn
sensitive	emotional
reserved	cold
enthusiastic	obsessed
persistent	importuning

The list could go on and on, but the lesson is clear—the use of adjectives can be misleading and unproductive. We suggest that, even though the issue is one of use or misuse of a trait, you *deemphasize discussion of the trait itself and concentrate on the incident.* It will usually be clear whether the incident was helpful or otherwise in getting the job accomplished, whether it had a positive or negative effect on company image or co-worker morale, or whether it represents an asset or a liability to the employee in his or her present job or future career. Even if it is *not* evident to both parties (boss and subordinate), fruitful dialogue is promoted by discussing the incident itself, alternative approaches, and ways to strengthen or suppress the particular type of behavior. Avoid debating the meaning of an adjective or the cut-off point between the productive and the nonproductive. We don't mean to imply that there will always be agreement as to the meaning or importance of the incident. However, if properly handled (as a problem-solving discussion rather than as an attack on the employee's individuality by the manager) this method of introducing traits and personality into the appraisal process can be helpful both to the organization and to the employee. We cautioned before not to attempt to change another's personality—it is only the individual who can do that. But if motivated by the knowledge that the chances for personal growth, achievement, and contribution will probably be increased if certain behavior patterns are changed, the employee may do just that!

Critical incidents are important not only in trait analysis but in the more "objective" measures of performance as well. In using them you must be quite selective in your screening to make certain that they are indeed "critical" in determining or reflecting performance. For example, to state that an employee "shows impatience with certain duties that are a part of the job" is merely to raise the question of whether the impatience hindered or actually helped in the performance of those duties. The use of critical incidents, filed over a period of months, must be in the context of the employee's overall performance. Only incidents that have produced one or more of the favorable or unfavorable effects covered in this unit should become a part of the appraisal. Managers must live with the fact that employees who are excellent in most respects may exhibit habitual traits that are a constant source of annoyance or irritation to the manager. But if you, the manager, cannot conscientiously say that the trait is hindering the employee's performance

interfering with the work of others

reflecting badly on the corporate image, or

hurting the employee's chances for personal and career growth

do not overemphasize its significance.

The critical incident method must be used with sensitivity and in a spirit of helpfulness to the employee. Managers must be sure that they are not concentrating only on the negative incidents, and must at all costs avoid overwhelming the employee with the feeling that big brother is watching every move.

CAN PER-SONALITY BE CHANGED? We have advised that you concentrate on incidents rather than traits in your discussions with employees on their approach to getting the job done. But note the possibility that by (1) feeding your perceptions of these incidents back to the employee promptly, (2) relating them in your discussions to job performance and personal advancement, *and* (3) rewarding changes in the desired direction by encouragement and other forms of positive recognition, you can help an individual change certain aspects of personality. Remember, however, that you are there to improve performance first, and that a campaign to encourage major personality changes can be a full-time job in itself. Concentrate on changing the single most significant type of behavior and keep the primary goal — improved performance — always in mind. An employee whose performance is good in all or most other respects is certainly worth this investment of your time. Only your own judgment can tell you how much time you and your organization can afford to spend on personal projects like this, and at what point it may become necessary to admit that you have an individual who is in the wrong job.[1]

---

[1] See Marion S. Kellogg, *What to Do about Performance Appraisal,* rev. ed. (New York: AMACOM, 1975) for an extensive treatment of appraisal in coaching, personality change, and termination of employees.

EXERCISE 4   1. In an appraisal discussion, how would you handle an employee mannerism which you find very irritating, but which is not significantly affecting job performance?

2. From your experience with your employees, describe a positive incident and a negative incident relating to the following traits:

Trait	Incident
a. Ingenuity	Positive:
	Negative:
b. Initiative	Positive:
	Negative:

    c. Cooperativeness   Positive:

                                   Negative:

    d. Positive
       attitude   Positive:

                                   Negative:

    e. Stability under   Positive:
       pressure

                                   Negative:

3. List the five traits, attributes, or characteristics which you consider most important in determining whom you would select to fill your next vacancy in a managerial position.

Commentary on Exercise 4

1. It is sometimes difficult to admit that an employee's performance is *not* being affected by a particularly irritating trait or personal mannerism. A negative halo effect (one which causes our whole estimate of a person to be colored by a single aspect of performance or personality) may be operating in such a case. You know the right answer when viewing this hypothetical situation, but it may not even occur to you when meeting the situation face to face. If you have an employee with an annoying trait, be especially careful to examine his or her performance dispassionately.

2. We will only comment on part d, "Positive attitude." This is such a broad generalization—really a cop-out from a serious attempt to describe a person's behavior—that you would have been entirely correct to refuse to answer that part on the grounds that it was meaningless. If you recorded an incident here, go back and try to find one or more specific traits that it illustrates.

3. The history of the trait theory of leadership shows that there is little correlation between leadership success and any single trait. There are some combinations that you would be wise to look for in a potential manager. Intellect, persistence, adaptiveness (that is, a wide range of styles, approaches, and coping behaviors to fit a variety of situations), inquisitiveness, energy, assertiveness, all might rank high on your list depending upon the demands of the job. It is important that you distinguish traits from skills and abilities learned through experience. The first are what the candidate must *be,* the second are what the candidate must *know* or *do.* Examples of the latter are "must be a shrewd judge of people," "must be able to weigh alternatives and reach sound decisions," "must have foresight to recognize potential obstacles," and so forth.

If you feel frustrated or dissatisfied over the outcome of this exercise, be prepared to feel doubly so if you discuss these matters with an employee without being thoroughly prepared. You need to double-check yourself to make certain that the critical incidents you are using really are critical, and that they have a real or potential effect on the employee's performance, co-worker performance, company image, or the employee's future.

You can avoid much argument and possible embarrassment, and still have a very productive discussion, by not attempting to tag your critical incidents with a trait-name at all.

UNIT 5

WHAT TO APPRAISE
MEASURES OF PERFORMANCE

We expect that many readers will breathe a sigh of relief at the prospect of dealing, finally, with results. These might seem to be much simpler and easier to appraise than the nebulous personality traits and idiosyncracies we have been considering in the preceding units. We wouldn't be doing our job, however, if we didn't raise a yellow flag at this point and warn you that there are several different types of results[1] that need to be measured and somewhat distinct approaches to measuring each type. We feel it necessary to raise this warning because of the mythology that has developed around MBO, leading to "principles" stating that if you can't measure the results of an effort directly you haven't set a proper

---

[1]This implies, of course, that there are several different types of *objectives* also. We will deal with this as we go along, but, if you wish to dig deeper, we refer you to Vol. II, Unit 5.

objective, and that you should not measure "activity," only "results."

We will cover indirect measurement of results (including the use of the critical incident) and the appraisal of activity in this unit.

If you already feel "up" on this aspect of appraisal, skip to the exercise at the end of this unit. If your answers satisfy you, continue with Unit 6. If not, you will profit by returning to this point and reading on.

For many tasks planned and executed in an MBO system, it is possible to measure and appraise performance by using countable or otherwise precisely measurable outputs or results. Table 1 contains some examples of this kind of output measure for several types of organizations. It also contains examples in which the results are stated in terms of critical incidents, and others in which the result is stated only in terms of an activity level, a project completion, or even the *initiation* of an activity. We will come back to these points later.

For now, note that we have included in the table output examples for a number of different key results areas. While the KRAs of these widely different organization types would certainly differ in some respects, for simplicity of presentation we have used only those KRAs that would be applicable to all the organizations represented. They are taken from a list recommended by Peter Drucker for general consideration by any organization.[2]

Your set of KRAs should be used as a checklist to avoid (both in objective setting and performance appraisal) the problem incurred when an attractive and favorable result in one area may by its very attainment cause deterioration in another area. For example, cutting the costs of maintaining a city's streets, the laundry equipment in a hospital, or the production equipment in a manufacturing plant could result respectively in deteriorating citizen relations, a rise in the cost of purchased or rented linens for the hospital, or a drop in capital productivity for the manufacturer. In terms of KRAs, an improvement in cost/profitability has been obtained only at the expense of performance in public

[2]Peter F. Drucker, *Management: Tasks, Responsibilities, Practices* (New York: Harper & Row, 1973), Chap. 8.

responsibility in the city and in productivity in the plant. The hospital situation illustrates another common problem of performance in which the favorable and unfavorable effects are confined to a single KRA, cost/profitability.

Of course it is rare in a complex system such as a large organization (or a system of KRAs) for a change in any subsystem to have absolutely *no* effect on other subsystems. Evaluating the quality of a performance therefore becomes a matter of balancing the positive effects against the negative ones. You will have to rely on your managerial judgment and detailed knowledge of your organization to help you decide whether any given performance is clearly positive in its overall effects, and to enable you to ask the appropriate questions of your employees when they propose their objectives for the coming appraisal period.

ROUTINE IM-PROVEMENTS VERSUS PROJECT COMPLETIONS

If we analyze the output measures shown in Table 1, we easily see that they express the accomplishment of two distinct types of objectives:

1. Those that require an improvement in performance against the continuing responsibilities of an individual job or of an organizational function

2. Those that require a significant project or innovation in order to gain a major improvement in operation, introduce a new product or process, or solve a major problem

Examples of type 1 are a reduction in customer complaints, lost-time accidents, employee grievances, machine downtime, and overtime; other examples include an increase in return on investment, more participation in the employee suggestion program, and greater compliance with federal Equal Opportunity guidelines.

The project (type 2) objectives are represented in Table 1 by various start-ups, "completions," and installations. In the final analysis, however, the difference between the two types is only one of degree. Improvement in continuing responsibilities is likely to come only as a result of a series of deliberate, planned actions, which differ from the actions needed for major projects only in

Table 1
Examples—Measures of Output or Results

Key Results Area	City Public Works and Recreation Departments	Manufacturing Plant Operations	Hospital Facilities and Operating Departments	Corporate Research & Development Division
Cost/profitability	Reduced cost per mile of paving Reduced cost per 1000 cubic feet of water distributed Clerical reduction from computerized tax bill preparation	Reduction in manufacturing payroll as percent of sales Annualized value of cost reduction projects completed Decreased production costs thru purchasing materials in bulk	Cost reduction from contracting floor waxing instead of internal Net saving in steam costs from high efficiency packaged boiler	Profit margin on new products introduced in last 5 years (rolling figure) Annual savings from automated analytical equipment Annual saving in production costs from development of substitute raw material
Market standing	(Output measures not generally applicable, but the incidence of citizen actions for secession, annexation, etc., may reveal the presence of "competition")	New product introduced into production successfully and on time Reduced frequency and severity of customer complaints on delivery service	Reductions in operating costs per patient day* Improvement in waiting time in emergency room*	Percentage of equivalent products judged equal to or better than competition Reduced average development time in lab prior to turnover to manufacturing
Productivity	Increase in percent operating time of refuse collection equipment Increase in number of games scheduled in municipal coliseum Increased interest return on idle revenue receipts	Reduction in downtime on production equipment Improvement in return on manufacturing plant investment Reduction in percent overtime to total hours worked	Increased room occupancy rate Reduction in idle time of lab technicians Revised layout of OR to improve use of space	Increased number of products handled per scientist via increased paraprofessional staff Installation of micro-processing facilities, doubling productivity of lab B
Innovations in product and service	Institution of heavy trash pickup at curbside once per quarter Start-up of minibus service for elderly and handicapped	Effective action in facilitating scale-up of new product from R&D Installation of "hot line" delivery service shortening delivery of orders received on Friday by 36 hours	Establishment of mobile cardiopulmonary emergency unit. Eleven probable "saves" in first 6 months Start-up of out-patient surgery facilities for selected cases	Successful development of product with unusual or unique features Development of computerized product design and materials selection

Employee attitudes and concerns	Union representation defeated by largest majority in five attempts Decreased citizen complaints about behavior of refuse collectors	Decreased percent of total employee grievances going to 3d step Reduction in lost-time accidents per million hours worked	Increased number of employee suggestions received per 1000 employees Decreased turnover ratio from 11.0% to 6.7%	Reduced absenteeism among lab technicians Installation of fire blankets, acid showers, and dispensary in high-energy lab K.
Management development	Two department heads accepted by ICMA Professional Development Society Exchange program initiated to rotate foremen into manager's office quarterly	Three promotions from plant operating management to corporate headquarters Installation of in-plant management development curriculum for engineers	Completed team-building workshop for department heads. Improved cooperation noted as result Three custodians promoted to foremen on completion of GED exam	Increased percentage of technicians enrolled in company-related courses at community college Project-team organization installed to provide opportunities for exposure to management problems
Public responsibility	Completed start-up of third-stage sewage effluent clean-up facility. Meets all clean water standards Completed EEO Affirmative Action training of supervisors	Installed cooling tower to recycle process water formerly contaminating Big River Added x-ray inspection equipment for detecting flaws in product. Screened out 15 potentially harmful units	Published and distributed brochure to public on preventive health in the home Enlarged waiting area, added snack bar and more comfortable furniture	Instituted hazard survey procedure during early stages of product development Started 3 year term as chairman of public policy study group on nuclear energy
Balance between long- and short-range objectives	Output measures of efforts directed toward this KRA are not likely to be seen except over a long period of time. We have included it here because it is necessary to consider it in asking the question on all current objectives, "Does pursuit of this objective detract unduly from the effort needed to ensure long-term health of the organization?" One output measurement that may be applied in all organizations is the percent of total effort expended on emergencies and for short-term benefits. The "correct" figure will be only a rule of thumb and will vary with the organizational mission.		

*Compared with other public or private facilities in market area their narrower scope, shorter time span, and greater informality. These actions become almost a part of the day-to-day job. As such, they can also be easily forgotten or subordinated to the paperwork, emergencies, and crises that are such a large part of almost any operating job.

This gives rise to two problems, one in setting the objective itself and another in measuring the performance of the individual or individuals responsible for it. We have already touched on the first when we stated in Unit 1 that *an objective is not complete unless accompanied by a plan of action.* This is especially important to remember in the case of an objective that involves an improvement in a routine or continuing area of responsibility, to reach or exceed an "indicator value" or "level of excellence." There is a strong tendency for boss and subordinate to agree on a "5 percent increase" in some level of performance, relying largely on faith, hope, and "the breaks" to achieve it. A backup plan is necessary to validate this type of objective. (This is less likely to be a problem in establishing a project-type objective, since action steps, milestones, network analysis, and other validation devices are more generally recognized as an essential part of project planning.)

The problem that arises in appraising performance against objectives based on faith and hope has two sides:

> In the case of *failure,* it is impossible to determine the reasons for failure without having specific action steps to review. The appraisal discussion may well degenerate into excuses and recriminations, or at best be inconclusive ending with an effort to redefine and validate the objective, which of course should have been done in the first place.

> In the case of *success,* the problem becomes one of deciding whether the employee deserves full or even partial credit for the achievement. Was it "the breaks" that were responsible? Or did action on the part of other employees produce all or some of the improvement?

Again, without the plan of action available for review, the already difficult process of conducting a rational appraisal or progress review becomes even more difficult. The credibility of the whole process is now damaged in the mind of the employee as well as in that of the manager.

Our emphasis on a plan of action does not imply that the employee should not be encouraged to develop *alternate* plans and actions to overcome difficulties as the job progresses. In some cases a review of the steps actually taken will show that they have little resemblance to the original plan. If success resulted, you will have learned a great deal about the ability of your employee to cope with unforeseen problems or to capitalize on opportunities for improvement that develop along the way. If the change in plan resulted in failure to reach the objective, you have the opportunity to explore the rationale of the employee's decisions. In either situation, the plan itself has enabled you to conduct a much more productive appraisal of performance and to learn much more about the employee.

Neither do we intend to encourage the establishment of improvement targets that have no "stretch," that is, ones that account with 100 percent certainty for every iota of improvement planned. If an employee has firm plans that can account for a 3 percent improvement in worker productivity, an agreed goal of 5 percent might be established, with the employee committed to finding ways to make up the difference. In appraising the results, you might assign a greater weight in your judgment of overall performance to the contributions the employee makes above the built-in level of 3 percent. If you suspect that an employee is holding back on ideas during the objective-setting discussion in an attempt to impress you later with a super performance, you will benefit by reviewing the commentary on Exercise 1B, question 5.

CRITICAL INCIDENTS

In Unit 4 we introduced the concept of the *critical incident* as a powerful and nondestructive way to attack the difficult problem of personality and its effect on work performance. We will now extend the use of this concept into result areas in which *output* has been traditionally hard to measure.

The results of some activities are so difficult to measure that the attempt to do so has been abandoned. But the activity often goes on, fueled by faith or maintained by the urge that keeps us from abandoning any kind of effort once we have staffed up for it. The difficulties may be more imagined than real, resulting from failure to exercise creativity in the measurement process or from the excessive importance given to quantification, which is often equated with measurement. Measurement "by the numbers" is not necessary to appraisal of performance, at least not in the short run.[3]

The critical incident (CI) is the tool that often fills the gap. We used CIs in personality assessment as indicators of the existence of a trait, style, or approach to getting the job done; we use them again in output measurement as indicators that the job is getting done, qualitatively, quantitatively, on time, or any combination of these. The main requirement is that the incident move the effort, in the judgment of the manager, toward the objective (or toward the level of excellence, whichever is appropriate). Some examples will illustrate:

Objective	**Critical Incident**
1. Completion of a major construction or development project	Solution of a problem that was a major obstacle to completion
2. Timely submittal of major capital appropriation request	Worked three weekends to regain time lost during emergency that arose
3. Improvement in managerial competence of staff	Delegated his authority *down* to a subordinate during his 6-week absence, rather than *upward* to his boss as he had always done before
4. Improvement in image of her department as a deadend for capable employees	Two promotions of subordinates to other departments during past 12 months
5. Improvement of plant image at corporate headquarters	Extremely favorable comments made by CEO following recent plant visit

---

[3]Ultimately, the results of achieving almost any goal or objective can probably be expressed in numbers. Often, however, these results do not become apparent until long after the performance appraisal of the individual, which is our concern here, has ceased to be important. Teaching excellence, for example, might be measured ultimately by the percentage of students reaching a specified level of income, or by the number who become Nobel prize winners. But, in addition to their lack of timeliness, the expenditure of effort needed to obtain such dubious measures makes the game hardly worth the candle in individual performance appraisal.

6.	Improvement in human relations competence of first-line management	Conducted role-playing sessions in human awareness for all supervisory people

These critical incidents provide definitive measurement against what are, in most of the above cases, qualitative rather than quantitative objectives. In addition, the positive recognition given to the subordinate for such examples of desirable behavior should act as a positive motivator—perhaps a stronger one than the establishment of a numerical goal, which always leads to the temptation to play the numbers game, often in ways that are difficult for management to detect.

Example 4 illustrates a point often made by purists in the measurement field, namely, that the two promotions out of the department should perhaps have been the objective rather than the somewhat nebulous "improvement in image." In other words, a useful way of setting objectives in difficult-to-measure areas of performance is to express them in terms of *making a critical incident happen!*

Example 6 above—the implementation of a training program in human awareness—will serve to introduce the final topic of this unit, the measurement of activity rather than results, a procedure that MBO authorities often look at askance.

ACTIVITY VERSUS RESULTS It is true that the purpose of the MBO system is to improve organizational results and not merely to promote a frenetic level of activity and busy-ness. It is also true that in retrospect many training programs seem to have done nothing more than keep the training staff busy. How, then, should we evaluate the suitability of the sixth critical incident cited above as a measure of performance? We suggest four questions you can use to evaluate an activity.

1. Does it reflect recognition and concern on the part of the subordinate for the problem?
2. Is it purposeful? That is, can it reasonably be expected to have an impact on the problem, or does it represent a logical step toward the solution?

3. Is it the first thought to come to mind, or was it selected as the most probable contributor to success from a series of alternatives?

4. Does it provide a basis from which subsequent measurements of results can be made?

If your answers to all four questions are affirmative, you are on firm ground in accepting an activity as an objective. The activity should lead to measurable results (questions 2 and 4). It will also tell the manager a lot about the employee. It should indicate an awareness of and concern over problem areas, and measure the employee's decision-making ability — the capacity to generate and evaluate alternative courses of action and to select the best one (questions 1 and 3).

Question 4 also forces the manager to think about continuing the monitoring of an activity after it is completed, until the desired results are obtained. Taking the sixth critical incident listed above as an example — the completion of role-playing sessions in human awareness for all supervisory people — we see this as an activity that might well produce affirmative answers to the first three test questions. The fourth question forces the manager to think about what the final measurements will be. These might include improved attitude survey results, or reduced frequency of grievances in units whose supervisors took part. Whatever the desired results, the manager must keep the completed activity under surveillance until results are produced. You might even include in the objective itself a statement of the type of *results* expected. However, it may not be possible to predict the extent or magnitude of the improvement at the time the objective is proposed.

In the final analysis, then, the theorists are right. Results *must* be the ultimate focus of any appraisal system. But the pragmatic approach recognizes the essential role of well-planned *activity* and that many tasks do not lend themselves to a complete or immediate focus on results.

The next unit will show how the principles we have discussed so far are incorporated into an overall performance appraisal system for the organization.

EXERCISE 5A

1. Table 1 contains output measures of three general types: (1) attainment of, or progress toward standards or levels of excellence in carrying out continuing responsibilities, (2) results of project work, and (3) critical incidents demonstrating performance in areas otherwise difficult to measure. Turn to the table and categorize each output as (1), (2), or (3). Place your answers on the table itself.

2. Some of the results in the table can probably be attributed to the efforts of one individual; others may come from the efforts of more than one person, or may be more appropriate as measures of the *manager* of the operation in which the results were obtained. Categorize the outputs as I for individual or M for group or manager. Place your answers directly on the table.

3. Some of the entries in the table reflect activity, not results, or results that are unclear. Examine all entries carefully and list below the ones in this category adding for each a statement of results that you feel would be appropriate and desirable.

Commentary on Exercise 5A Your categorizations should be substantially as listed here. (A = activity only.)

KRA	City	Plant	Hospital	R & D
Cost/Profitability	(1) I (1) I (2) I	(1) M (1) M (note a) (2) I	(2) I (2) I	(1) M (note a) (2) I (2) I
Market Standing	(3) (note b)	(3) I (1) I	(1) M (2) I	(1) M (note a) (1) M A
Productivity	(1) I (2) I A (2) I	(1) M (1) M (note c) (1) M	(1) M (2) I (2) I	(2) M (2) I
Innovations	(2) I A (2) I A	(3) I (2) I	(2) I (2) I A	(2) I A (2) I A
Employee Attitudes and Concerns	(3) M (2) I	(1) M (1) M	(1) M A (1) M A	(1) M (2) I
Management Development	(3) I (note d) (2) I A	(3) M (2) I A	(2) I (3) I	(3) I A (2) I A
Public Responsibility	(2) I (2) I A	(2) I A (2) I	(2) I A (2) I A	(2) I A (3) I

Notes

a. These are valid measurements of overall performance, used primarily in the appraisal of the overall R&D function or its manager, rather than of individuals or managers at lower levels. For these measurements to be truly effective, a trend should be established and evaluated, since a single measurement does not provide sufficient information for appraisal.

b. Critical incidents may on occasion, as in this case, come from outside the organization. The person being evaluated need not always be the principal actor in the incident that reflects his or her performance.

c. As worded here, the three examples in this cell concern the manufacturing plant as a whole, therefore, they are best applied to evaluating the effectiveness of manufacturing management as a whole. If defined more specifically, they might be suitable for evaluating individuals (I).

d. This example might be viewed as a critical incident reflecting the two department heads' concern for their own growth, and therefore used to evaluate them as individuals. However, since the management development KRA refers primarily to the efforts of management at all levels to assure the supply of future managers for the organization, the individual to whom this specific measurement applies is the city manager.

Comments

1. The point of this exercise is not to determine whether an individual or a manager should be evaluated by a particular output measure, (as a matter of fact, in a number of cases the manager of the component *is* the individual being appraised), but to examine the way in which middle- and higher-level managers (i.e., managers of managers) are appraised. Obviously, since the higher manager retains responsibility for all activities under him or her, the manager must be appraised on all these activities. It would be both cumbersome and meaningless, however, to appraise him or her on the results of every project, critical incident, or routine operating improvement. It is common practice to combine such results into general measures like those coded M in the commentary on the preceding page. These then become measures of the overall effectiveness of the manager's operation, recognizing that planning, selection, staffing, and policy decisions, and the operating climate that he or she establishes have a great influence on that effectiveness level. Every manager, at whatever level, is also subject to individual measurements, particularly in the management development, innovation, and public responsibility areas where the manager's personal effort and concern serve as models for subordinates or have a substantial effect on corporate image. Another individual measurement, which must be reflected in a manager's objectives, is performance against the commitments made to subordinates during the appraisal and progress review discussions — commitments to provide the employee with support, guidance, information, and development opportunities. We will cover this in more detail in Units 7 and 8.

2. We may have seemed severe in categorizing certain examples in Table 1 as activity-oriented rather than as concrete results. Here is our rationale for each example:

Reduced average development time in lab	Be careful! What are the results — perhaps nothing better than poorly developed products?
Increase in number of games scheduled	A good start, but one on which judgment might be deferred until the next appraisal period — were the games played? Probably yes, if project was the result of public demand, but not if "numbers" was the motivation.

Institution of heavy trash pickup Startup of mini-bus Successful development of unique product Computerized product design Exchange program to rotate foremen In-plant management development program Project team organization Published and distributed brochure on health in the home Enlarged waiting area Startup of outpatient surgery	All these are potentially worthwhile activities and specifically directed at their KRAs. There is little reason to doubt that they *will* produce the planned results, but *completion* per se is only the first measurement. These certainly add to the appraisal of performance, but should be monitored over a period of time. Conceivably some of them might be dropped or discontinued if they are not utilized or do not produce the desired results.
Completed EEO/AA training Instituted hazard analysis	Watch out for ''compliance only'' in response to consumer and other legislative pressure. What follow-up is planned?
Installed cooling tower	No results indicated. Does it or will it work at the planned level of effectiveness?
Increased number of suggestions received	Indicative of stimulation of employee interest, but what is their value? If not implemented, could do more harm than good.
Decreased turnover from 11 to 6.7 percent	Numbers look good, but are they merely the result of fewer ''quits'' because of slack job market?

EXERCISE 5B   Since you should be using all three types of output measures in your own objective-setting and appraisal processes, it is beneficial to know the kinds of situations they fit best and to gain some practice in recognizing their form and content. The above exercise was a warm-up. Now, using your own job, and whatever KRAs are appropriate, list one result you have personally achieved (or which your organization can take credit for) in each of the KRAs. If you can, list three for each KRA, one in each of the three categories: (1) ongoing performance improvement, (2) project results, and (3) critical incident. Use the form on the next page.

   As an alternate exercise, try doing the same thing for a subordinate whom you have recently appraised.

   (Having done the previous exercise, you should be able to judge your own work at this point; we will provide no further commentary.)

UNIT 5

My KRA	Category and Description of Results	
	1	
	2	
	3	
	1	
	2	
	3	
	1	
	2	
	3	
	1	
	2	
	3	
	1	
	2	
	3	
	1	
	2	
	3	

UNIT 6

DEVELOPING AN APPRAISAL SYSTEM

Up to this point we have considered appraisal as a part of the MBO process (Unit 1), given you a chance to assess the current status of your own appraisal process (Unit 2), discussed the psychological bases and the development of the results-oriented appraisal system (Unit 3), and introduced you to the complexities of measuring both the how and the what of an employee's performance (Units 4 and 5).

We are now ready to put all this together into a procedure that you can use or adapt for your own organization. The elements of this procedure, which we will discuss in some detail, are (1) the day-to-day "real-time" appraisal, (2) the progress review, (3) the overall performance appraisal and development review, and (4) the salary review and discussion. These are summarized in Table 2. If, after reviewing the table and the forms to which it refers (Figs. 3, 4, 5, and 6), you feel that your present procedure provides an adequate framework for applying the prin-

Table 2
The Elements of the Appraisal Process

	Day-by-Day	Progress Review	Overall Performance Appraisal	Salary Review
Purpose	Improve on-the-spot control and guidance.	Review current progress, determine needs, reset objectives.	Retrospectively review performance and long-range career planning.	Communicate salary action.
Form	Informal conversations, job-site visits and observations.	Scheduled formal meeting.	Scheduled formal meeting.	Ad hoc meeting.
Frequency	As need and opportunity dictate, but at least once each week.	3 to 6 months.	(Note a)	(Note a)
Inputs Documentation and data	Routine reports, conversations, rumors.	Work Planning Guide,* Detailed Action Plan,* job description,* written objectives, action plans, Work Objective Progress Review.*	Career plan, Progress Review Forms.*	Applicable data from Progress Review Forms,* and overall appraisal.
Typical needs and problems	*Employee's* need for boss's interest and support; discuss resource allocation and bottlenecks encountered and progress made; need for access to new information. *Boss* needs verification of reports, knowledge of employee's motivation.	Need for replanning future effort, and for concentration and corrective effort on key objectives.	Need for mutual overall review of employee progress and performance on job and in personal development.	Need for tangible recognition, equitable treatment, and optimum use of discretionary funds.
Content	Conversation on current problems, needs, and job status.	Detailed examination of performance vs. objectives; objective setting for next review period, discussion of "how" as well as "what."	Summary of performance, strengths, needs for improvement, progress against career plan; considerable emphasis on "how," relationships with others, etc.	Discussion of salary action and supporting reasons; employee expectations.
Outputs Documentation	Normally little or none; occasional memos or entries in employee file by manager.	Revised objectives and action plans; newly revised Progress Review Form.*	Revised career plan; summary of overall appraisal; revised Work Planning Guide,* completed overall appraisal.	Personnel records.

Table 2 *(Continued)*
The Elements of the Appraisal Process

	Day-by-Day	Progress Review	Overall Perform-ance Appraisal	Salary Review
Results desired for employee	Immediate help on problems, improved rapport with manager; opportunity to display knowledge.	Formal commitment of manager to expedite and assist; opportunity to air problems and accomplishments.	Recognition of overall contribution and potential; more purposeful self-development program.	Tangible recognition of performance, feeling of equity.
Results desired for manager and organization	Critical incidents; first-hand knowledge of job and employee; strengthened relationship.	Review and maintenance of progress against objectives; performance correction.	Fulfillment of management development responsibilities; development of needed skills.	Motivated subordinate; equitable relationships among work force.

Note a:

Highly discretionary; the frequency of salary reviews and overall appraisal depends on status of employee, nature of job, and other variables. See text.

*These documents appear as Figs. 3 to 7.

ciples and techniques we have covered so far, and can produce the desired results, you may wish to skip to Units 7 and 8. In those units we will discuss the techniques of structuring and carrying out a productive progress review or appraisal discussion, and the techniques available to management for encouraging and monitoring employee and manager development. In any case, work through Exercise 6. It will help you decide whether or not to skip this unit.

CONTINUAL APPRAISAL Any formal planning or review activity carried out by an organization can easily become routine, static, and unproductive if it is only carried out periodically. This principle applies whether we are talking about the annual budget, the 5-year plan, or the review of performance against objectives. Each of these procedures must be *used* over the period to which it pertains if it is to provide any degree of control over events. The day-to-day appraisal has several purposes. For the manager it provides a degree of on-the-spot, concurrent control of performance against objectives set in the formal periodic progress review discussions, as well as data for use in subsequent discussions with the employee. Both these purposes can be important to a manager, but especially to one who is new in the position or who has untried or marginal employees. The data gathering should not, of course, be done in a secretive or snooping fashion, nor should the data be withheld and then unloaded on the unsuspecting subordinate at the next formal review. (There may be *patterns* of behavior, however, which can be analyzed only over a period of time or over an extended series of incidents, and which may be brought out at that time without being unfair to the employee.)

Daily phone conversations with employees, visits to their places of work, observations made in meetings, comments made in the margins of reports and memos may all seem so routine to many managers that they do not consider them part of the appraisal process. Their potential for achieving the purposes we have mentioned, however, is significant and easily overlooked. These casual contacts can become more purposeful and productive if they are considered in that light. For the employee they provide an important ingredient in job satisfaction — the timely recognition of his or her trials and triumphs and a sense of the boss's interest and concern not only for the employee as an individual, but for the importance and dignity of the job itself.

The way these contacts are made, the sources of information developed, and the amount of time the manager spends on them depends on individual style and the situation. We will not presume to specify any rigid format or frequency, nor even attempt to "teach" you to use them. Neither do we suggest that you formalize them in the sense that we recommend formalizing the progress review, appraisal, and, to some extent, salary discussions. (By *formalize* we mean plan and schedule the activity, commit both parties to carrying it out, and give it the status that will result in mutual commitment to the success of the outcomes and to honoring the agreements made.)

However, we strongly urge you to compare the percentage of time you spend behind your desk sending or receiving written communications with the percentage spent observing, listening, and otherwise interacting with your people on their "turf," giving each the attention he or she needs. What you do with the results of that examination can be important not only to the effectiveness of your appraisal system, but to your success as a manager as well. Get out from behind that desk!

THE PROGRESS REVIEW The heart of the MBO appraisal system and the element that most distinguishes it from other, more conventional systems is the progress review. This must be a regularly scheduled event of top priority for both manager and subordinate. We recommend a quarterly review during the early stages of the introduction of MBO. A less frequent review may be appropriate for your top performers or for those whose objectives are laid out far in advance by the nature of their work (and perhaps automatically reviewed on an almost continual basis through your project control procedures); however, we suggest that progress be reviewed at least semiannually. Even though the work itself may be progressing well and on schedule, a discussion of *how* the job is being done, with emphasis on personal needs and development, is usually appropriate. It is also likely that boss and subordinate can benefit from a review of the economic climate, changes in the market, and other environmental factors that often require changes in the objectives for the coming period. *The review, then, should involve a close look at the objectives themselves, not merely the performance against them.*

The employee should use these opportunities to raise issues that he or she sees as impeding progress, even when coping successfully with them—and the manager should accept responsibility, where it is clearly indicated, to assist in setting up conditions or providing resources that will improve performance. However, only after both parties have thoroughly examined the situation to determine whether diligent exercise of the employee's own responsibilities could lead to a solution should the manager step in. The manager who too readily assumes responsibilities that should be the employee's will soon find it impossible to manage effectively, as employees beat a steady path to the office door with problems for the boss to solve or, perhaps even worse, the more self-sufficient achievers begin to shun the unwanted help, setting up a potentially disastrous barrier to communication.

The outputs of the progress review mechanism, then, are:

Review of performance

Review and resetting of objectives

Help for the employee where needed

OF TIME AND PAPERWORK A common and very understandable reaction of managers to the prospect of a quarterly review with each employee is one of discouragement. They question the practicality of the process in view of the time involved and the "inevitable" mountain of paperwork that will accumulate. In case you are sharing that feeling right now, let's stop for a moment and consider these potentially very real problems.

First, ask yourself the question, "If I were to spend one hour every 3 months with each of my employees, and do the follow-up work on the commitments I make to them, what activities would I have to give up?" If you answer that question honestly and objectively, you are almost certain to find that there are activities on which you should spend less time than you do now. In any event, there are probably few activities that have a higher priority for a manager than reviewing job performance and personal progress with employees and maintaining a climate and a structure that will help them do their jobs. Certainly the MBO system of management is a demanding one. But concentrating on the more important duties can make it less demanding.

Second, beware of making a ritual out of the appraisal process. If all appears to be going well, and you have established a continuing and genuine rapport with an employee, you should be able to touch bases very quickly at the appointed time, make any needed adjustments in objectives, and conclude the review in minutes rather than hours. We do *not* recommend that you *skip* the scheduled review, however. To do that would diminish the stature of this important event and lead to bad habits. It is preferable to agree to decrease the frequency on a formal basis, but this also has its disadvantages unless the parties retain the option to call more frequent meetings should either see a major problem developing.

Experience will teach you the optimum frequency of reviews. If the "soap opera syndrome"[1] is noted, by all means analyze the "ho hums" to determine whether reviews are scheduled too frequently or lethargy has set in on the job-site.

One reason for dull, long-drawn-out reviews is the failure to be selective about the objectives scheduled for review. Remember

---

[1] In these TV and radio dramas, it is possible to miss as many as a dozen episodes and still be fully aware of what is going on. Daily listening or watching quickly becomes a boring ritual, though the habit prevails even if nothing new is learned.

the Pareto principle — the 20/80 rule we cited in Unit 1 — and devote the time to the key objectives. There will be an opportunity to review progress on the whole job during the overall performance appraisal session described below.

Paperwork is another matter. The only rule to follow, since there is no way of eliminating paper altogether is to keep documentation simple and make it concise and selective. Again, limit it to the key objectives and use a telegraphic rather than a narrative style. As we suggested in Unit 1, use the output of your management information system whenever possible, especially in reporting the level of performance against routine or continuing objectives.

Forms should be simple and brief. Our preference is for a blank piece of paper with guidelines in the form of notes or a checklist to help ensure coverage of the important points. Examples of this approach are shown in Figs. 3 and 4. Fig. 3 is a form that can be used for recording performance against work objectives; Fig. 4 is a form for recording performance against personal development objectives. We offer these samples as alternatives to the usual four- to eight-page forms which imply that the user should fill them. Much time and file space is used up in recording noncritical information.

As shown in Table 2, these forms can serve as both the inputs and outputs of the progress review discussion. They can also be derived from the Work Planning Guide, shown here as Fig. 5, which we recommend for use in the initial phases of an MBO system, but which also can be used as input and output to and from the overall performance appraisal session. The guide for use of this blank piece of paper is shown symbolically at the top, with notes added to provide a checklist for the user. The flow of the thought process which you should use in completing this form follows the reasoning in Unit 1, with the broad consideration of major responsibilities, tasks, or KRAs, leading to the ultimate or long-range measures of performance ("indicators" or "levels of excellence"). These in turn lead to the establishment of short-term objectives and the action planning needed to validate or back them up. The Detailed Action Plan (Fig. 6) is a more detailed statement of the action steps required for complex plans. It is designed to facilitate note taking during progress review sessions.

FIGURE 3
Progress review:
work objectives.

Job Holder:	Reporting Period
Job Title:	From_____ To_____

Objectives (See note 1)	Results (See note 2)

NOTES FOR FIGURE 3   **Note 1**

Restate objective from Objective column of Work Planning Guide (Fig. 5) if used, or record directly from results of progress review discussion.

If entire objective is not to be achieved within the reporting period, add events from action plan that *were* to be achieved during the current period.

Note 2

Results may be in terms of quantitative or qualitative output, timely and purposeful activity, or critical incidents. (See Unit 5.)

Note any reason for major deviation from plan. Corrective action should appear as a new objective.

Consider modification of objectives if changed circumstances so warrant.

Note any needed changes in information reporting system, added resource or support requirements, or release of resources unnecessary to assure objective accomplishment. Commitment to added support or resources should also appear in *reviewer's* objectives for next review period.

Work out any additions, deletions, or revisions for next reporting period objective statement. Set a date for submittal and review of next objective statement, if not done during progress review session.

UNIT 6

FIGURE 4
Progress review:
management and
personal development
objectives.

Job Holder:

Reporting Period

Job Title: From_____ To_____

Objectives (See note 1)	Results (See note 2)

NOTES FOR FIGURE 4   **Note 1**

Objectives should be taken from Work Objectives Progress Review form (Fig. 3) or from the overall performance appraisal. These objectives may relate to behavior changes that will augment work performance, or may be the result of career development planning.

If appropriate, express in measurable terms (quantity, quality, time, cost); if not, *describe activity* which should lead to desired results. For example:

> "Will develop 10 year career progression plan with specific job assignments requested for discussion with manager by February 1, 19___."

> "Will enroll in MBA program and complete one course towards completion, in fall semester, 19___."

> "Will attend the 1-day seminar on group leadership scheduled at Central University on March 18."

Note 2

Results should be measured not only against objective criteria of accomplishment (e.g., "completed on time"), but should also reflect reviewee's subjective evaluation of change resulting from described activity.

If objective is stated as a training activity (see note 1), work out a plan for utilizing training and maximizing benefit in the work environment. Action on this plan may be added to next joint revision of reviewee's objectives.

FIGURE 5
Work planning guide.

Job Holder:

Job Title:

Major Responsibility (See note 1)	Levels of Excellence (See note 2)	Objectives (See note 3)	Plan of Action (See note 4)

NOTES FOR FIGURE 5

Note 1   Major responsibility

Derives from the individual's job description (Figure 7).

Starts with a *verb form* describing the activity (e.g., "To produce . . .," "To process . . .," "To formulate . . .," etc.).

Has an *object* of the action (e.g., "applications," "checks," "meals," "supervisors," etc.).

Contains *qualifiers* describing *why, when, in what manner,* etc. (e.g., "in order to maintain . . .," "at 3-month intervals," "to conform to . . . standards," "through use of hired contractors," etc.).

Use 20/80 (Pareto) rule in deciding whether or not to list.

Note 2   Level (standards) of excellence*

Answer the question, "Under what conditions can it be said that this responsibility is being carried out satisfactorily (excellently) (unsatisfactorily)?"

May not always be achievable within next review period.

Are best (but not necessarily) expressed *numerically,* with *limits* (e.g., "maximum of 0.1% rejects," "maximum cost of $0.80 per meal," etc.).

May need to be stated in terms of *timeliness* (with dates), *quality* (with definition), or *quantity* (as a time rate) (e.g. "all monthly cost reports submitted within 5 days after closing," "quality of service so that client complaints do not exceed 5 per month," "50,000 documents processed per shift," etc.).

Must not merely indicate present level of performance, unless specific action is needed to maintain that level.

Note 3   Objectives

Are stated as a *target,* or desired *status.*

Are quantitative, when possible to express in numbers.

Should involve *reach, stretch,* or *progress* toward or beyond indicator levels.

Should be *realistically achievable* (i.e., backed up with action plan).

Must be *output-* (or *results-*) oriented, not activity-oriented (but see text of Unit 5).

Represent a *joint commitment* between manager and subordinate.

Are limited in number, covering *major responsibilities* (but there may be more than one for a single major responsibility).

Must contain time limits (e.g., "by November 19__").

Should meet all other requirements of sound objectives, as listed in Unit 1.

May refer to Levels of Excellence (e.g., "attain 0.1% reject level by . . .," "decrease meal cost from $0.86 to $0.82 in first half 19__," "get halfway from current level to indicated level of excellence by end of second quarter 19__," etc.).

Should each carry a priority ranking with respect to all other objectives of the individual preparing the form.

Note 4   Plan of action

Who will do *what, when,* and *with whose help.*

If complex action is required, refer to Fig. 6, "Detailed Action Plan."

*Skip this column when objectives are expressed as completions of project activities. (See Unit 5.)

FIGURE 6
Detailed action plan.

Objective:

Prepared by:

Date:

Milestone Event (note 1)	Completion Date	Man-Months		Other Resources	Review (note 2)	
		No.	Source		Date	Status and Action Required

NOTES FOR
FIGURE 6   **Note 1   Milestone events**

Simple action plans involving few steps may be defined directly on the work planning guide, Fig. 3.

State events as the completion of essential steps in the actions required to achieve the objective.

Critical path or PERT techniques may be helpful in identifying all essential steps and the need for concurrent as well as sequential action.

Include man-months and other resources obtained from outside the department or component in order to define contributory responsibilities of others needed for achievement of the objective.

Contributory responsibilities or borrowed resources must be multilaterally agreed on by all managers involved. Unilateral inclusion of these is appropriate only in preliminary, tentative planning.

Note 2   Review

Two reviews are provided for each milestone event. The first should be sufficiently in advance of the planned completion date to allow for corrective or supplemental action, if needed. The second should follow the planned completion date.

Employee and manager should both maintain records of reviews.

Additional reviews may be entered on a blank sheet if required.

Two questions frequently asked are: "Who prepares the forms?" and "Who gets copies?" The first is a matter of choice. Our own preference is for the employee to prepare the results column of the progress review form (with a copy to the boss for preview) as close as possible to the date of the forthcoming progress review, so as to reflect the current status. This is consistent with the principle that self-measurement is best. Ideally, the employee knows more about his or her performance than anyone else. (If it turns out that the boss has a number of surprises for the subordinate, both individuals should ask themselves why this information was not placed in the hands of the subordinate first!) The boss will have retained a copy of the form listing the objectives agreed on during the previous review on which he or she may have recorded pertinent incidents or observations during the review period. These may be discussed with the employee during the forthcoming review, but the critical incidents should already have been discussed informally.

To accomplish all this, only two copies of the progress review forms are necessary. There is a strong tendency for the manager to ask for an additional copy or two to be passed up the line. Managers should resist the temptation to take this easy way out in preparing their objectives for the next higher level. If they do not, MBO will create a mountain of paperwork for higher levels of management to deal with. This multiplication of forms can be avoided if managers summarize and evaluate their components' performance, rather than merely pass along everything generated by the individuals who report to them. The specific objectives and results of progress reviews are normally a matter of discussion between the two principals only. The overall performance appraisal, on the other hand, is often reviewed and augmented by the next higher manager, and in most organizations a copy is also kept by the personnel office.

Before we leave the progress review, we wish to reemphasize the importance of formalizing the commitment of the manager's action to help or remove obstacles from the path of the employee's performance. These commitments to action should appear as objectives on the manager's Progress Review: Work Objectives (Fig. 3) for the coming period. Managers of managers are well advised to look for and question the absence of such commitments on the part of subordinate managers.

THE OVERALL PERFOR- MANCE AP- PRAISAL

Progress reviews serve to keep efforts concentrated on the important key objectives and the need for improvement by the organization and the individual. If, however, reviews are carried out as we have recommended using the Pareto Principle and limiting the number of projects and improvement efforts included, some aspects of the job will not be subject to joint scrutiny during the year. The overall performance appraisal, with which you are already probably familiar since it is in widespread use in most organizations, fills this gap. In many organizations, the appraisal process is by and large limited to this (usually annual) event.

The overall performance appraisal does more than merely pick up the loose ends left over after the progress reviews. It makes it possible to take stock of the relationship between the incumbent and the whole work situation, away from the inevitable pressures that exist when the boss and subordinate are discussing progress on key objectives. The performance appraisal is both retrospective in focus and oriented toward the longer-range future of the employee and the job itself, rather than toward progress on currently important tasks.

The philosophy and content of this major element in the appraisal process will become clear to you from the following outline of the issues considered in a typical appraisal format designed to be executed at 18- to 24-month intervals.

I. Performance

    A. What has been accomplished?

        1. Against all specific job responsibilities

        2. In all key results areas

    B. What overall strengths and weaknesses have been evidenced?

    C. What action is needed by employee and manager?

    D. Where else might strengths be used?

II. Knowledge and Personal Characteristics

    A. Assess knowledge of technology in present field and position.

    B. What knowledge of other fields may be useful in present or future positions?

    C. Assess knowledge of your organization, of management as a job, of social/political/environmental forces.

D. Assess personal attributes and use of them. Typical questions may be:

1. Is there evidence of high ethical and moral standards?

2. Are personal and narrow departmental interests often set aside in favor of organizational concerns?

3. Stable under pressure? Able to maintain sound positions against force of popular opinion?

4. Perceptive of pitfalls and fallacies in own and others' ideas?

5. Adaptable to new situations?

E. What strengths and weaknesses have been noted?

F. What action is needed by employee? By manager?

G. Where else might strengths be used?

III. **Effectiveness in Getting Things Done**

A. As an individual contributor. Ask such questions as these:

1. Is a strong success drive noted? Is the employee willing to pay the price of success?

2. Does he or she stick to the job in spite of drudgery and obstacles?

3. A self-starter, requiring little supervision?

4. A calculated risk-taker?

5. Does he or she make effective use of time on and off the job?

B. In working with associates and others. Ask such questions as these:

1. Is the employee a good listener?

2. Respected by associates?

3. Persuasive?

4. Alert and sensitive to reactions of others?

5. Can he or she take issue with others' views without incurring antagonism?

6. An effective communicator of ideas?

C. As a manager of the work of others. Ask questions about:

1. Clarity with which component objectives are communicated.

2. Anticipation and action on opportunities.

3. Level of goals and standards for self and subordinates.

4. Soundness of policy formulation.

5. Quality of personnel selections.

6. Clarity in defining job responsibilities and work assignments.

7. Effectiveness in use of salary as an incentive.

8. Action taken to bolster weak spots in organization.

9. Participation of subordinates in decision making.

10. Respect in which employee is held by subordinates.

11. Efforts to resolve conflict by negotiation or consensus rather than by force of will or position.

12. Quality of performance appraisal system for subordinates.

13. Action taken to correct performance problems.

14. Quality of performance measurement systems.

D. What action is needed by subordinate and manager in each of the above areas?

IV. The Development Plan

A. Long-range: What direction? Continued professional development as a higher level specialist? A move into or out of management? A staff assignment? Move to another functional area?

B. Short-range: Improving on the present job.

C. What joint actions are required by manager and subordinate?

The above outline may be used as a guideline or checklist in conjunction with the now-familiar blank piece of paper to function as the record of the overall performance appraisal. The lists of questions used to examine personal attributes and effectiveness as an individual, a team worker, and a manager may be expanded, and rating scales can be applied to each answer, but if you are alert you will recognize that if this is carried too far you will wind up with nothing more than the long-discredited attribute appraisal described in Unit 3. *The reason for the questions is not to syn-*

thesize a performance rating from the answers, but to use the answers to pinpoint the areas in which development or corrective action is needed—and then to go on and specify that action.

In contrast to the preparation of the progress review forms, the manager should take the lead role in preparing the overall appraisal, although it is helpful to have the reviewee also prepare a self-appraisal for comparison purposes. Differences in perception are more likely to be revealed and resolved in that way than by relying solely on the employee questioning the prejudgments of the boss. It is especially important to get these types of issues resolved, because the salary review is necessarily dependent on the reviewee's total contribution over an extended period of time, which is what the overall performance appraisal is designed to measure.

THE ROLE OF THE JOB DESCRIPTION

An essential piece of documentation in the well-designed performance appraisal system is the individual job description. It provides the basis for the employee's short- and long-range objectives as inputs to the progress review and as benchmarks for overall performance appraisal.

As indicated in Unit 1, the MBO system demands a more sophisticated statement of the scope and purpose of the individual's job than is found in the usual job description. An actual example of an MBO-oriented job description is shown in Fig. 7. Major features of this document are the clear definition of performance criteria in all major areas of responsibility, and the guidance it gives both the employee and the manager in formulating measurements for use in determining performance.

TITLE:	Manager of Production Engineering	DATE:	2/21/___
DIVISION:	Manufacturing		
RESPONSIBLE TO:	Plant Manager	LOCATION:	Houston

I. Purpose

The manager of production engineering is accountable to the plant manager. The section is responsible for providing and maintaining manufacturing facilities and processes for production of new and existing products at optimum cost and quality levels.

The section is a vital link in the prompt transfer of newly engineered products into full-scale production and is a major contributor to the company's reputation as a responsive, cost-competitive, and quality supplier. It is the company's first line of defense in protecting the safety of employees and customers from the hazards of the production processes and of poorly manufactured products, respectively. It carries primary operating responsibility for the protection and conservation of the impacted environment of the plant.

II. Position Scope and Responsibilities

A. *Functional and Managerial Responsibilities*

Design and install all processing and handling equipment and other manufacturing facilities for new products, expanded production of existing products, environment control, and general plant improvements.

Provide for design of equipment for the above purposes by utilization of engineering resources outside the section, internal or external to the company, whenever the work involved can be done more economically elsewhere.

Revise and standardize existing processes for improved control and quality of all products, and improve labor and machine utilization upon consultation with the manager of industrial engineering and the plant superintendent.

Reduce manufacturing costs by any of the means above, by improvement of material and energy balances, and by service to the manufacturing section to solve production difficulties.

Introduce into plant operation experimental products in cooperation with the engineering division and manufacturing section.

Provide for all maintenance and safety services to the Houston plant.

Coordinate and compile plant capacity figures periodically and initiate action to provide necessary increases.

FIGURE 7
Statement of
Position Scope
and Purpose
(pp. 99–102)

Provide estimates of facilities expenditures, manufacturing costs, and other applicable technical data for use by sales and engineering divisions in preliminary evaluations of new products.

Take an active part in plant cost reduction and safety programs, as a member of management.

Maintain an awareness of new technical developments and regulatory requirements within the industry and apply these whenever practicable.

Provide for continuity and growth of plant capability by selecting and developing competent personnel to carry out the work of the section.

B. *Relationship Responsibilities*

Delegate to subordinates the fullest possible measure of authority for decision making and contribution to profits, and provide a climate in which employees may discuss their plans and problems and receive advice and counsel, without relieving them of their decision-making and other operating responsibilities.

Coordinate the resources and efforts of the section with other sections and with the engineering and sales functions by participation in business team and other activities.

Use the functional services and appraisals of staff divisions as their concentration and specialization upon functional aspects enable them to provide such aid.

Make fullest practicable use of informal "channels of contact" to supplement channels shown on the organization chart, and encourage other members of management to do likewise.

III. Position Authority and Reservations of Decision-Making Authority

Standard Practice Instruction PE-4, entitled "Delegation of Authority," establishes reservations of decision-making authority from the manager and subordinates.

The manager has the authority and responsibility to make recommendations as to subject matter on which decision-making authority has been reserved, to secure decisions thereon, and to take appropriate action thereafter.

IV. Criteria and Measures of Performance for the Position

The criteria and measures of successful performance by the manager of production engineering will include the following items.

A. Effectiveness of activities to provide required production facilities for new and existing products, as measured by:
1. Thoroughness of periodic audit of future needs, and changes in effective plant capacity figures
2. Extent of lost business because of late facilities installation*
3. Success of toll production operations when required
4. Reduction of overtime and/or addition of capacity by cycle, utilization, and yield studies*
5. Adherence to engineering and environmental standards of quality in production of new products

B. Effectiveness and timeliness of cost reduction efforts, as measured by:
1. The percentage of actual and budgeted total cost reduction achievement contributed by the production engineering group*
2. Specific improvements in yield, spoilage, manufacturing cycle, and labor and machine utilization obtained through production engineering activities*
3. Reduction in utilities consumption and maintenance costs achieved by engineering improvements*
4. General extent of participation of the group in cost-reduction program activities
5. Long-term trend in planned production cost levels for all products

C. Effectiveness of maintenance and plant engineering services, as outlined in the position responsibilities and measured by:
1. Reduction in machine breakdown time*
2. Effectiveness of cost control against budgets*
3. Performance against established preventive maintenance inspection programs and parts inventory limits*
4. Action in cases of emergency breakdown
5. Coordination of maintenance activities with production schedules
6. Anticipation of need for changes in and additions to utilities and services to the plant
7. Operating difficulties encountered in new equipment, and the effectiveness in elimination
8. Control of cost in connection with plant appropriations*

9. Labor and space utilization efficiencies achieved by sound design and drafting

10. Status of labor relations in the maintenance area

[In the original, measures of each of the following criteria were also present. These measures are eliminated here for brevity.]

D. Effectiveness of quality-improvement activities

E. Quality of service provided to other sections and to management, in capital budgeting, production cost estimating, facilities design and layout, and other service responsibilities

F. Effectiveness and extent of participation in professional activities and others involving assimilation and adoption of new engineering knowledge and techniques.

G. Effectiveness of personnel selection and development, including delegation of responsibility and authority

H. Effectiveness of control and use of assigned financial and other available resources in the company

I. Quality and timeliness of decisions and action on all responsibilities, including recommendations where decision-making authority is reserved

J. Thoroughness of hazard analyses conducted on all products and processes, and effectiveness of design work in reducing safety hazards to employees and customers

*Numerical standards of excellence based on current conditions and needs will be set and maintained until revision is indicated. Review will be annual.

THE SALARY REVIEW

We include the review of the employee's salary status and planned salary action as a part of the appraisal process, because to many (perhaps most) employees and managers alike salary level and performance level are inseparable. There is, however, good reason not to develop expectations on the part of the employee that every overall appraisal session is going to close (or open) with the good or bad news about a salary increase for the coming year. The inevitable impact of the salary action, favorable or unfavorable, is certain to divert the employee's attention from the discussion of improvement needs and development plans.

We recommend the separation of the two discussions, or at least that the overall performance appraisal be carried out free of the diversions created by a discussion of salary. The converse is not true, however. When the salary review is conducted, it is not desirable nor even possible to avoid reviewing the results of the most recent performance appraisal session. Such a review will reemphasize the reasons for the salary action, the strengths and accomplishments being rewarded, and the performance deficiencies or development needs that may inhibit salary growth.

The salary review meeting should not be formally scheduled far in advance. It is best handled (promptly) when the salary recommendation is approved, to avoid raising expectations and to avoid the possibility of diminishing the importance of the progress reviews and the overall appraisal meeting in the employee's mind. It should be made clear that when a salary action finally does come about, it is the result of the cumulative outcomes of the other discussions.

We will have more to say about the relationship between salary and performance in Unit 9. First, in Units 7 and 8, we will suggest ways to make the various discussions more effective in improving performance and cementing the relationship between manager and employee on a one-to-one basis.

EXERCISE 6A For each of your subordinates (or for yourself if you have none), determine the frequency you think is appropriate for each of the three appraisal or review sessions and enter the date (month and year) on which you would hold the next session. Be prepared to explain differences (or your own needs).

	Frequency		
Employee	**Progress Review**	**Overall Appraisal**	**Salary Review**

Commentary on Exercise 6A

Progress reviews are probably best held every 3 to 6 months, with newer employees and those on critical projects at the lower end of that range. It is also helpful when first implementing an MBO system, to start off with more frequent reviews (some managers hold them monthly) and decrease the frequency as the skill level increases. Recall the soap opera syndrome to remind you that "too many" can be just as damaging as "not enough."

The period between overall performance appraisals varies from 12 to 24 months in most organizations. The fast-track, high potential employee can make use of the guidance that the appraisal provides at more frequent intervals than a mature employee who has reached a stable level in the organization. This type of individual should not be put on the shelf, however, and 2 years should be the maximum period between serious discussions, so that the almost inevitable backsliding can be held to a minimum, and every opportunity is provided to stimulate continued growth. It is rare not to see some slackening—or at least leveling off—of performance as the retirement years approach, but this deterioration can be unwittingly accelerated by neglect of the appraisal process. "Shelf-sitters" are there because they are *put* there by management. Remember that work is important to self-respect. The fact is that long-service employees are often overlooked when the important projects are handed out, and often neglected in the communication process. The overall appraisal we have described addresses both these issues and can help keep your long-service people off the shelf.

The frequency of the salary review is so heavily influenced by the individual organization, its salary plan, and the status of the employee that it is difficult to set limits. One thing we should caution against, however, is the *annual* salary adjustment. This often creates false expectations on the part of the employee, and encourages managers to give token raises so that "she (or he) won't have to wait 2 years," even when a raise is not really warranted. It is also helpful to have the flexibility to reward an outstanding accomplishment immediately, even when the raise comes only 6 or 9 months after the last one, or to be able to say to an employee, "I am deferring your salary review for 3 months so you'll have the opportunity to improve your performance."

We hope that you heeded our rule that a progress review and a salary review should not normally be conducted at the same sitting. This rule, like most others, is only a guideline, and if a progress review session consists largely of a report on the solution of a major problem by the employee, it may be acceptable and beneficial to indicate to the subordinate that you are recommending a raise.

In all your responses, you should consider relating these new procedures to your present system, seeing especially how the changes might fit into your present schedules for annual budgeting, annual updating of the long-range plan, and other existing routines.

EXERCISE 6B Compare your present appraisal system with the one shown in Table 2, and record below the features of your system that you feel may be deficient. Suggest ways to improve your system. (It may help to review your responses to Exercise 2A and B in identifying needs and weak points.)

Element	Deficiency	Suggestions
Day-by-day appraisal		
Progress review		
Overall performance review		
Salary review		

Commentary on Exercise 6B

Your analysis is likely to indicate either (1) a lack of one or more of the elements, or (2) deficiencies in either the content or output areas. In the first case, you should review the rationale given in Unit 6 (especially if you decided to skip it and went directly to this exercise), and then draft a procedure for your organizational component that will correct the deficiencies (or a memo to yourself if the deficiency occurs in day-to-day contacts!). In the second case, Units 7 and 8 may be of help. They contain suggestions on how to make the all-important interactions between manager and employee more productive, both in terms of performance and future growth.

If your present procedures tend to combine elements—for example, the progress review and the overall appraisal, or the overall appraisal and the salary review—you should consider the pros and cons discussed in the preceding unit and in Units 8 and 9.

UNIT 7

CONDUCTING THE PROGRESS REVIEW AND OVERALL PERFORMANCE APPRAISAL DISCUSSIONS

We have stressed several times in this three-volume series our conviction that *an improved one-to-one relationship between managers and subordinates is the real difference that MBO can provide to the well-run organization.* Some organizations adopt MBO because they have lost their sense of purpose and need a good hard look at where they should be going and how they can get there. These organizations realize that they are in trouble and look to MBO for help. Others find themselves in much better shape, both technologically and structurally, but see opportunities for improving the productivity of their employees by making them more concerned and cooperative members of the organization.

George Odiorne, one of the fathers of MBO, once made the

109

statement that an individual's loyalty at work is to the smallest group of which he or she is a member.[1]

Think about your own work experience before accepting that as gospel, but the chances are that you will agree. Your loyalty is probably to your boss and the group of coworkers in your organizational unit. In the well run, results-oriented organization—the MBO organization, if you will—loyalty to that small group is by definition loyalty to the overall purposes and direction of the parent organization.[2] In that group, at whatever level in the hierarchy, the boss is the one who sets the tone (which depends heavily, in turn, on his or her loyalty to the next higher boss)—and that tone is transmitted, for better or worse, by the individual relationships between the boss and each subordinate. True, a part of the boss/subordinate relationship in a work group is determined by the way in which the boss handles the group *as a group,* but the real key to *that* is, in turn, how each member retains his or her individuality in group processes.

The manager/subordinate relationship, then, is a crucial ingredient in the success of MBO, and becomes increasingly important as the organization realizes the structural benefits of MBO and the emphasis shifts to the humanistic. Because of space limitations, we will not attempt to conduct a course in human behavior and motivation, but will concentrate on the specific skills needed to make the periodic progress reviews and overall performance appraisal discussions more effective. You will also find these skills useful in your day-to-day contacts, in conducting salary reviews, and in problem-solving discussions of all kinds.

INTERVIEWING AS A PRODUCTIVE FORM OF DIALOGUE

We will use the term *interview* in characterizing the various kinds of discussions involved in the performance appraisal process. In doing so we recognize the risk that the word may conjure up a picture of a one-sided question-and-answer session controlled by the interviewer, who may even use verbal trickery to elicit information from

---

[1] Speaking to a management development group on "Personnel Management by Objectives" at Dulles International Airport, December 7, 1973.

[2] Dissidents and maverick groups are an exception, of course, but in an organization that operates under objectives and measures progress in terms of them, such a group cannot operate unknown to the manager. How the manager handles such a situation is a good test of the abilities and skills we discuss in this and the next unit.

the interviewee. This is not the name of the game! We choose "interview" simply because the word is more useful than others such as "appraisal," "review," or "discussion," which are found in the literature on the subject of face-to-face dialogue. (See the brief annotated bibliography at the end of this volume.)

The interviews we are talking about are designed to do something for two parties who share a common interest — getting the job done well so that both organization and individual may grow. Some of the techniques we describe may seem manipulative at first. We are nevertheless sharing them with you, your boss, and your subordinates, confident that, once you are *all* aware of these techniques, you will all benefit. You will be able to read one another's nonverbal signals, to use the probing techniques to help get to the bottom of a problem, and to recognize and overcome the inevitable resistances you'll encounter.

SETTING UP THE INTERVIEW

The type of session we are dealing with is important enough to require that its status be clearly understood and accepted by all parties. The appointment should be made well in advance and honored by the boss if at all possible, even in the face of conflicting demands on the part of higher management. Interruptions by the boss's boss during the session should also be avoided whenever possible. Once the sanctity of the progress review or appraisal session has been properly established in the organization, the higher-level interrupter, when told a session is in progress, should respond by saying, "I understand. I'd appreciate a call as soon as they are finished."

Setting up the appointment should remind both parties to do their homework in preparation. The manager should organize the pertinent data he or she has gathered. The subordinate should do likewise. (See Unit 6 for suggestions on preparing the paperwork.) After reviewing the data (including the subordinate's updated progress review forms, if you decide to use that format), you may decide that certain items should be stressed. In that case, give the subordinate the courtesy of letting him or her know in advance, by means of an informal agenda. The meeting itself is no place to spring surprises if you are serious about strengthening your relationship.

Whether or not to prepare a complete formal agenda is a matter of choice. We are inclined to advise against structuring the session in this way because it tends to promote rigidity in the discussion. It is wise, however, to prepare a guide for the use of both parties outlining the objectives of the discussion, but not specifying in detail how they will be reached. We will return to this when we consider the specific types of meeting below.

WHEN YOU INTERVIEW, BE SURE YOU COMMUNICATE

Interviewers in all fields have found certain principles and techniques useful in understanding what goes on in the one-to-one communication process and in reaching conclusions helpful to both parties. Getting all the facts, feelings, and viewpoints into the open, and arriving at useful conclusions in an interview is a matter of reducing the factors that hinder communication and utilizing those that facilitate it.[3]

Inhibitors of Communication

The *pressure of time* is a notorious inhibitor. A hurried interview, or one punctuated by the interviewer's nonverbal signals of impatience — glancing at one's watch, failure to control outside interruptions, or obvious preoccupation with the next interview — is unlikely to achieve any useful objectives. The best way to avoid this is to give the meeting the stature it deserves. Even when time contraints are severe, selectivity and the use of an interview outline can help minimize the pressure.

Threat to the ego of either party is another powerful inhibitor. The interviewee will naturally try to avoid giving information that is unflattering, or inconsistent with his or her self-image or role. The tactics used subconsciously in this situation may include depersonalizing ("anyone would have done the same thing under the circumstances"), rationalizing ("What else could I do?"), or misunderstanding the question, and minimizing the importance of the event. We bring these things up not just to alert managers to the hang-ups of employees, but to alert both parties to these tendencies. Remember that the manager will become the interviewee in a higher-level discussion. But regardless of that fact, even the interviewer,

---

[3]See Raymond L. Gorden, *Interviewing: Strategy, Techniques, and Tactics,* rev. ed. (Homewood, Ill.: The Dorsey Press, 1975), pp. 70-95.

especially one who is new to the give-and-take relationship with subordinates that MBO demands, may have ego problems. The manager who is inexperienced in interviewing may feel the threat of *loss of control.*

The control-conscious manager is likely to show this concern by the manner of questioning. Watch for *leading questions* that imply that the questioner already knows the answer, *double-barreled questions* (asking a second question before the interviewee has had a chance to answer the first one), *frequent interruptions* that change the direction of the questioning, and *assumptive statements* that draw conclusions or infer something which was not stated by the interviewee. At the same time, the employee may be reacting to the control imposed by the manager. Subconscious attempts to avoid control include vagueness, attempts to "turn the tables" by asking the manager questions or by repeated requests to clarify, interrupting the manager before he or she has a chance to finish a comment or question, and monopolizing the time by engaging in long, rambling narratives.

Some of these symptoms are aggravated by the pressure of time on either one or both the parties. Whatever the cause, the danger is that these concerns will dilute the conscious attention which each participant must give to the interview objectives in order to maximize communication. It is difficult to understand others when we are wrapped up in our own concerns.

Imperfect memory is an inhibitor that may also affect the type of interviewing we are concerned with. Memory problems on the part of the appraiser or interviewer are the most common source of what has been called the *recency bias,* in which the overall appraisal is colored by events or incidents that happened within a few weeks of the appraisal period.[4] This bias is seldom deliberate, but it appears so often that we caution you again as a manager to record and file, no matter how informally, critical incidents and other indicators of performance on a continuing basis.

---

[4]Another form of bias is the *halo effect.* Here one event or attribute — favorable or unfavorable — causes the rater to grade the individual similarly on a number of *other* performance characteristics or attributes. This is not as likely to be a problem in a results-oriented progress review, but can affect a manager's judgment when preparing an annual (or less frequent) overall appraisal.

The employee's memory often becomes a problem when the two parties attempt to reconstruct events chronologically — often a necessary part of analyzing the development of a problem on the job. We will describe an approach to surmounting this communication barrier in the section on the sequence of questioning.

Facilitators to Communication

One of the most important facilitators of open, frank, two-way discussion is the expectation on the part of both persons that the interview will indeed be conducted in that manner. But it takes more than a verbal statement on the part of the manger to create openness. Asking for frankness in an interview is a poor substitute for exhibiting it in day-to-day relationships. It is unlikely that a normally closed, secretive, close-to-the-chest manner on the part of the boss will encourage frankness on the part of the subordinate in a progress review or appraisal discussion. Such a manner communicates to the

Drawing by Stevenson;
© 1977 The New Yorker Magazine, Inc.

"To all employees: It has been recently observed that when Mr. McCutcheon says 'How are you?' certain employees have taken this simple greeting as an invitation to 'let it all hang out.'"

employee more powerfully than any words that frankness is something undesirable, unpleasant, or embarassing for the boss, and as a result it may become so for the subordinate as well.

As a manager, one of the best rules you can follow to encourage frankness is to avoid giving the impression of infallibility. Admit your mistakes openly, identify opinions as such, show a willingness to change your mind when faced with evidence contrary to your beliefs, and do not be afraid to apologize when wrong. Such behavior shows that you want and can tolerate frankness — and errors — on the part of others. It takes a reasonable degree of security and self-confidence on the part of a manager to treat his or her employees in that way. You are singularly unfortunate if you are working for a boss who does not have that sense of security and confidence!

Recognition of the employee as an equal in the discussion is another strong facilitator of productive communication. It helps if the boss gets out from behind that huge psychological barricade — the desk — and assumes the same spatial relationship (see the brief discussion of proxemics below) with the employee he or she would assume with a VIP who was invited into the office. Recognition and understanding of the problems that the employee may be facing on the job, as well as his or her accomplishments, also help communication and motivate performance.

The review and appraisal sessions have the potential to provide two additional facilitating influences on free communication if they are handled well. These are the opportunity for *catharsis* and the chance for a *positive payoff*. These factors operate, respectively, (1) to encourage the interviewee who has something to get off his chest to open up, and, (2) to facilitate communication because the interviewee sees that personal benefits may accrue from being open. A well-planned interview should encourage an employee who needs help from the boss to ask for that help and to participate in the problem-solving process. If your reviews are seen as sources of help and as productive outlets for the employee's feelings about the job, they will be successful in achieving those purposes.

Nonverbal Communi- cation A well-documented result of many research studies is that much of what is communicated between two people is transmitted by means other than words. (You can readily confirm this without being a skilled researcher by astute observation and analysis.) Such esoteric terms as *proxemics, kinesics, chronemics,* and *paralinguistics* have entered the vocabulary in recent years to describe the many types of nonverbal communicative behavior (much of it unintentional) that facilitate or inhibit productive interaction.

We will dispose of the first three types very quickly. *Proxemics* is the study of the spatial relationships between two communicants. The "proper" distance between the two persons is a function of the culture and of the nature of the communication. Most research on proxemics has been done in informal or social "stand-up" situations and the conclusions do not generally apply to the interviews in our setting. However, we emphasize again that placing a desk between the manager and an employee probably creates an artificial distance that is greater than the optimum. Placing the two participants on adjacent sides of a work table allows greater closeness and a sense of equality, and also allows both to refer to any data that is not available in duplicate.

Kinesics is the study of *body language,* the movements and positions that convey the emotions and feelings of the parties. Skill in interpreting kinesic data is most important to the professional interviewer engaged in social work, clinical psychology, and similar activities. However, the interviewer in our setting should be aware of just a few common and easily recognizable indications of tension and uneasiness. Persistent loss of eye contact with the interviewee is one, "white-knuckled" interlacing of the fingers of both hands another. A third is the rhythmic tightening of the jaw muscle easily visible in the cheek just forward of the earlobe. All or any of these may indicate that it may be helpful for the interviewer to back off, take a short break, or drop the topic under discussion and return to it later.

Chronemics is simply the study of the pace of the interview (as set by the interviewer) and the use of the silent pause. A slow deliberate pace is less likely to convey a feeling of tension and anxiety on the part of the interviewer or to produce those same feelings in the respondent. Failure to take this into account can easily lead to spiraling escalation of tension in both parties or, in some cases, to the psychological withdrawal or even breakdown of the interviewee.

Silence on the part of the interviewer can either increase or decrease the anxiety of the interviewee depending on how it is used. We will return to this later when we discuss probing as a technique.

Paralinguistics is the study of the way in which words are spoken. We include it here as a nonverbal form because the meaning of the words themselves or combinations of them are changed drastically by the way they are emphasized or inflected. As an exercise to demonstrate the changes in meaning by emphasis, take the sentence, "He'd never accept a bribe." Repeat it aloud four times, placing the emphasis successively on each of the four key words. The first rendition absolves the subject but implicates someone else; the second is a clear statement in support of the subject; the third and fourth imply other types or degrees of wrongdoing on the part of the subject.

To test the power of inflection in conveying meaning, try pronouncing aloud the word "yes" to indicate successively disbelief, desire for further information, anger, understanding acceptance, condescension, impatience, and haste. Many other emotions and feelings can be "tried on" for practice, but those listed are especially pertinent to the progress review/performance appraisal setting.

The cues that tone, emphasis, and inflection supply to the listener are broadly recognized and produce more response than those described under chronemics, proxemics, and kinesics. (They are also useful in circumstances in which some or all of the latter are not, such as on the telephone and in settings that make continuous observation of the interviewee difficult.) These cues are conveyed by facial gestures as well as by tone and verbal emphasis; a nod, a smile, or a frown can convey interest, encouragement, puzzlement, or rejection or acceptance of an idea.

There is no substitute for the understanding of the employee by the manager and vice versa; for example, the employee may know from experience that when the manager frowns he is most likely mulling over an idea and not rejecting it or the employee. The manager, on the other hand, should learn from the responses of each individual, which employees can be exposed to the full range of expression, verbal and nonverbal, without hurting communications and which cannot. You should be thoroughly forewarned by now that there can be problems in this area. We supply a bibliography in Unit 10, in which you may find material to help you develop nonverbal skills more thoroughly. We continue at this point with a discussion of the more substantive areas of the interview.

Developing a Topic: The Funnel and Inverted Funnel Sequences

The way you get into a subject with your employee is significant in determining whether the inhibitors are minimized and the facilitators strengthened. The *funnel sequence,* in which a broad topic, issue, or problem is discussed first, and the details are developed as the interview progresses, is the normal and preferred approach. The interviewer may be eager to find out about a particular critical incident connected with a major project. However, there are advantages in first asking for a general response, with a question such as, "How are things going on the X project?" This provides recognition (a facilitator) and diminishes the ego threat (an inhibitor); first, the employee is implicitly given credit for being on top of the project; second, he or she is not "diminished" immediately by the thought that the manager suspects that something is going awry at the nuts-and-bolts level. The funnel sequence also provides the manager more immediate evidence on how well the employee is handling project X and on what his or her thought processes are. Since this sequence normally stimulates the employee to respond in detail, there is also less likelihood that the manager will have to interrupt frequently with detailed questions in order to elicit the information. Finally, starting with a question related to the objective being measured, rather than with details, is likely to satisfy better the employee's need for catharsis. Thus the funnel sequence generally fits the inhibitor/facilitator model.

The *inverted funnel sequence* also has its uses in some situations. Where the objective of the interview is to generate a broad solution to a specific problem rather than to probe the details of performance against a broad objective, it may be less of an ego threat to start with specific incidents and symptoms and work toward a broad, inclusive solution.

Open and Closed Questions

Just as the funnel sequence is generally the more useful of the two techniques described, the *open question* is clearly superior to the closed question in stimulating two-way communication. The open question usually begins with one of Rudyard Kipling's "six honest serving men" — what, where, when, how, who, and why — presented here not in the order in which they appear in the famous poem, but in the order of increasing threat to the interviewee and roughly in the one in which they might be used in a funnel sequence.

They are called "open" because they do not force an answer. The *closed question,* on the other hand, is presented in a form that usually allows only two answers, generally "yes" and "no." A *loaded question* is a question which may appear open at the start, but which limits the answers to those wanted by the questioner. For example, "In your opinion, who is at fault here . . .?" (so far so good — a bit threatening, but still open) ". . . Product Development or Production?" (loaded!). In a situation like this, an interviewee alert for cues may reply, "I guess I'd have to say Production," whereas a more truthful and ultimately more productive answer might be "Well, neither really!" You may get the latter answer to that heavily loaded question, but if you do, it's more than you deserve!

We mentioned the *leading question* earlier in an unfavorable context (one in which the question implies that you already know the answer, whether you do or not). Another form of the leading question is a challenge to the interviewee offered without any ulterior motive. This is helpful in bringing to a close the inverted funnel sequence. The facts are now all on the table and the alternatives explored. Now is the time to challenge the interviewee with a leading but open-ended question, for example, "How do you think we had best proceed?" Note that this is much less of an ego threat than if you had decided to offer the same challenge as the opener in a funnel sequence.

In most of what we are saying here, the implication is that the interviewee needs the help that an interview like this can offer. Fortunately, your more independent and achievement-oriented performers will be in less need of help. They will already have decided on their course of action before the progress review or appraisal discussion begins, and will undoubtedly be turned off if you attempt to practice these techniques on them too assiduously. On the other hand, even such self-starters need recognition and feedback to confirm their achievements. Only you can decide on the proper balance for each of your people.

Probing   Probing involves the use of questioning to help the interviewee develop or recall the desired information. In many cases, it is used in paralinguistic form (a nod of the head, an "uh-huh") to create a permissive silence that encourages the interviewee to continue developing an idea or narrative. This silent probe is often enough to maintain the flow of information. If not, a neutral expression of interest, understanding, or attention will help ("No kidding!" "Wow!" "I see," "Hmmm," etc.) Probing is also needed for elaboration ("Tell me more about that."), clarification ("I don't quite understand. Tell me again about . . .") or recapitulation ("Take me through the major action steps again.")

If you are alert, you will recognize that we have again presented a series of techniques in an order that gradually increases the threat to the interviewee—and again we urge you to analyze your own employees and your own manner of questioning in advance to predict the reactions you may evoke.

The more common error in reviewing progress and appraising performance is not to appear threatening to your employees, but to miss opportunities to probe; as a result, you may fail to bring underlying problems and feelings to light or to stimulate creative thinking about alternative solutions.

Note Taking and Recording

Note taking during the interview should fit your own style and preferences. It has little inhibiting effect on most interviewees, but may divert your attention from important nonverbal cues and signals if you overdo it.

A common question is whether or not to use a tape recorder. Under conditions of mutual trust, the consensus is that this will generally have little or no inhibiting effect on the communication process. However, we think that if you rely on a tape machine to do your note taking for you, you will conclude very quickly that a prohibitive amount of time is involved in transcribing, editing, and pulling out the essence of the conversation.

We do recommend, however, that you use a recorder when carrying out the brief practice sessions that appear as exercises at the end of this and the two following units. This will be very helpful in assessing and discussing your use of paralinguistics, your development of topics, missed opportunities to probe, and other things which even a third-party observer might overlook or forget.

Following Up

Since one of the overriding purposes of the progress review and the overall performance appraisal is to close the loop on the MBO cycle, follow-up is crucial to the success of the process, and a review cannot be considered complete without it. A major output of these interview sessions is *action.* The formal commitment to action is recorded on progress review forms (Unit 6), or in whatever alternative form you choose to adopt. If these commitments are not made in writing as part of the interview itself, be sure to set a date for completion at the close of the session. We will return to this subject as we consider the two types of discussion separately.

THE PROGRESS REVIEW

We have recommended that a very general outline, or interview guide, be used to shape the progress review discussion, specifying only the objectives or desired outputs of the discussion and not a detailed structure. A suggested interview guide follows. Note that its headings suggest questions that can serve as the wide end of the funnel in a normal approach to the interview sequence.

Desired outputs (see Table 2)

Definition of progress against the individual's major objectives

Understanding of major problems or obstacles preventing progress, whether individual or organizational

Recognition of significant contributions made by the employee, and of needs for support

Establishment of new objectives to meet improvement needs

Revision of objectives where evidence indicates the need

Recommendations to higher management on organizational objectives, priorities, and resource allocation

Understanding of what needs to be done, when, and by whom

Joint commitment by both manager and employee to implement new and revised objectives and plans, and to make recommendations

The interview guide is also useful in judging the degree of success or effectiveness of the progress review in retrospect. Use it for that purpose. (It will be useful right away as a basis for a critique by yourselves or your observers following the practice sessions in Exercises 7, 8, and 9, which use the progress review as the simulated situation.)

We do not rule out a more structured approach for those who prefer to follow a sequential outline. An example from the literature, shown in Figure 8, follows a question-and-answer format, which uses the individual's major objectives as a starting point and is meant to be repeated as each successive objective is considered.

THE OVERALL PERFOR-MANCE APPRAISAL This event, occurring as it does with a much lower frequency than the progress review, and covering a much broader scope of activities, calls for a more structured approach to ensure full coverage. The outline and suggested questions for the overall appraisal that

FIGURE 8
What happens in MBO performance review?*

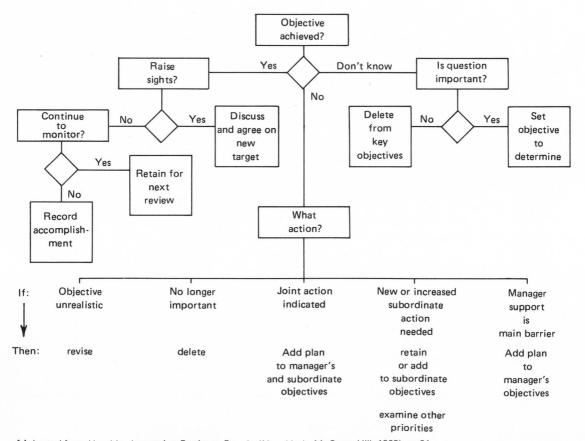

*Adapted from Humble, *Improving Business Results* (New York: McGraw-Hill, 1968), p. 91.

appear in Unit 6 will give you a good start on an interview schedule. The major topic headings are also useful in reviewing the effectiveness of the outcomes, just as the interview guide can be used in conjunction with the progress review.

The heavier emphasis on personal growth, development, and career planning that characterizes the overall performance appraisal calls for more introspection on the part of the employee than was needed in the case of the progress review. As a result, you may, as a manager, find that the appraisal session calls for more patience and helpful probing on your part, as well as considerably more time. Your inputs are important, too, especially your knowledge of company-wide opportunities and career paths, and of the many ways in which employee development can be fostered both on and off the job. We will examine a number of these in the next unit.

EPILOGUE   We have stressed interviewing skills very heavily in this unit — perhaps so heavily that you are ready to throw up your hands in despair — there is so much to learn!

Well, take heart. Even the best of the professionals have problems, as news columnist Sander Vanocur pointed out in a *Los Angeles Times — Washington Post* syndicated column that appeared on December 14, 1976. Commenting on an interview between another newsperson and President-elect Carter, Vanocur emphasized two points — the *failure to listen* and the dangers of maintaining an artificial *status difference* between interviewer and interviewee.

As an example of failure to listen, he cited a point in the Carter interview at which the President-elect was about to describe the period of self-examination and religious renewal that followed his defeat in his first gubernatorial campaign. The public wanted to know more (so, presumably, would a manager exploring an employee's philosophy of work), but the interviewer cut him off and changed the subject. Said Vanocur, ''. . . [the interviewer] was either not listening to what Carter was trying to say or thought it of no great importance.''

Vanocur, who is himself an accomplished interviewer, goes on to advise ''. . . the secret of good interviewing . . . is that the interviewer, in an effort to bring forth the interviewee's personality, must withdraw rather than advance on the person being interviewed.''

Vanocur's second point (here paraphrased so as to be directed at an audience of managers rather than at a TV news star) is that the higher your presumed status as interviewer relative to the interviewee, the harder you must try not to get in the way of information and of the person you are interviewing.

Interviewing skills and attitudes take years to develop. Even the best interviewer sometimes overlooks the important points made by Vanocur. We encourage you to work on improving your skills in the art.

EXERCISE 7   With a coworker (or with your boss or a subordinate) read the following situations. By agreement, or the flip of a coin, assign one person the role of manager in a situation of your choice and the other that of subordinate. Allow the "manager" 5 minutes to prepare an agenda.

Carry out the discussion as indicated in the situation, utilizing the principles and techniques we have covered, and try to achieve the desired outcomes depending on the situation. Supply yourselves beforehand with any blank forms (Figs. 3, 4, 5, and 6) you feel you may need.

Feel free to improvise reasonable questions and answers. The tests of reasonableness are whether or not the questioner would normally expect to get an answer in real life, and whether the answers will bear up under such questioning. Keep the discussion forward-directed to encourage yourselves to think of solutions to problems (rather than alibis). In your solutions, commit yourselves to actions that would be feasible in real life in your organization as you would like to see it — but explore their feasibility in your role enactment with your coworker.

When you have finished, switch roles and conduct the discussion over again, or move on to another situation taking new roles. There is no time limit. Continue as long as the discussion is productive, then criticize each other's contribution, and switch roles.

If a third person is available, he or she may act as an observer, and may give you and your partner some additional insight into your role performance. Where three of you are involved in this way, it is a good idea to rotate through three situations or repeats of the same situation, so that each may have a chance to take all three roles.

As our commentary at the end of this exercise, we have posed a series of questions on each situation that a good discussion should have raised and answered. If you are taking the role of observer, you may refer to this now to get an idea of what to look for as the discussion proceeds.

As you simulate this real-life situation, try to put yourself in the role you are taking. Rely more on your own feelings and reactions, and less on the role as described. Try to avoid looking at the situation description or referring to it in such terms as "but it says here . . .," "Are we supposed to assume that . . .?" "I don't understand what they mean by . . .," and so on.

Situation 1   One of you is the civilian manager of an engineering unit in the U.S. Army Corps of Engineers and the other the engineer assigned to writing technical manuals on flood control and environmental protection. The manager is committed heavily to employee development, partly because of pressure for more effectiveness from the Office of Management and the Budget, but also because he has a strong personal feeling that one should make the best of one's own talents, and wants the engineers to do the same. The engineer, on the other hand, takes little interest in advancement and even less in spending time away from his family to attend night classes or seminars or to do the heavy studying that goes with such programs. The engineer's work is excellent in quality, quantity, and timeliness, in fact, much better than the average engineer's. You are about to carry out the first overall performance appraisal the engineer has had in 18 months.

Situation 2   Technically and according to all the quantitative measures of performance used to monitor achievement, the employee is making excellent progress against the current set of key objectives. The first 3-month progress review promises to be a good one. The boss has noted, however, a number of rather disturbing things, which, added up over the 3-month period, seem to be worth discussing. The employee, whose output consists of instructional materials, has the secretarial pool up in arms because of her constant last-minute demands for reams of copy "to be done yesterday." This appears to be having a significant bad effect in slowing down the work of other professionals, whose work often has to be set aside to accomodate her demands. She is also domineering and aggressive in her relationships with both secretaries and professionals. If better planning were done, this would not be a problem, because her objectives and milestones were set 3 months in advance, and more effective use of her time would have allowed a smoother flow of output.

   The employee feels under great pressure to produce, being the newest person in the group, and the boss bears a good share of the responsibility for this, since he is under pressure himself, although he doesn't feel responsible for the employee's abrasiveness. He feels that the employee may be taking on too many jobs and doing too much, but finds it very difficult to discourage one of his best performers. The boss would like to ignore the secretarial problem, but the other professionals are beginning to complain since they, too, are under pressure to produce.

The employee has indicated a real desire for constructive feedback on how she is doing. Her main concern, which the boss realizes, is not to be "last to arrive, first to leave" in this "dog eat dog" publishing business, and she believes that the best defense is a good offense.

It is time for the progress review.

Situation 3   Both boss and subordinate recognize that running the customer service and complaint operation is pretty much a response-oriented job, subject to unpredictable demand and allowing very little project-type work in the major improvement category. As a result, the emphasis has been to maintain measurable achievements (such as the percentage of emergency orders filled within 36 hours) at a consistently high level compared with the competition, as reported by the sales force. After a year of the new MBO system, customer service is beginning to be looked upon as a status quo operation, and at the forthcoming annual performance appraisal session the boss has indicated to the employee that they need to spend some time discussing the future direction of the operation. Conditions don't appear to the employee to be conducive to this because of frequent crises, the tyranny of the telephone, and the constant importuning of the salesmen who want special action to satisfy their customers, but she is willing to discuss possibilities for action if the boss can come up with any ideas.

Commentary on Exercise 7

The following list of questions will give you a reading on how well and thoroughly you conducted the discussions. Answer them together with your partner. The questions may also be used as a checklist for observers to use during the role-taking session.

Refer to the list of desired outputs for the progress review (Unit 7) and the outline of the overall appraisal session (Unit 6). Were the outputs appropriate to the situation realized? If not, why not? Poor interview planning? Lack of an interview guide or outline? Loss of control by the interviewer? Too many closed-end questions? Others?

Did the interviewer show good use of the principles of chronemics and proxemics we covered in the text?

What kinesic or paralinguistic events did you notice as observer? (Tell the two principals about them.) Did the interviewer also notice? Was there a visible change in his or her behavior as a result?

How successfully did the interviewer avoid time pressure and ego threats? What specifically did he or she do to minimize these barriers?

Was a helpful rather than a judgmental attitude maintained by the interviewer? What incidents illustrate this?

What positive benefits from self-development did the interviewer stress to the employee in Situation 1? What *negative* results did he or she bring up, if the employee did not respond? Did the two come to an understanding? One that would be satisfactory in a real-life situation of this kind?

How did the interviewer approach the personality trait of the employee in Situation 2? Was it discussed as "aggressiveness," "pushyness," "abrasiveness," or as some other designated trait? Or was it handled as a description of undesired behavior? Did the interviewer admit his or her possible part in contributing to the situation?

How effectively did the interviewer in Situation 3 initiate exploration of opportunities for improvement in the employee's crisis-ridden activity pattern? Did the employee request, or did the interviewer offer help of any kind?

For maximum benefit from these exercises, repeat the discussions, rotating the roles among participants, until you are satisfied that all significant alternatives have been proposed to correct the problems.

UNIT 8

PERSONAL AND PROFESSIONAL DEVELOPMENT

It has been said that "all development is self-development." This is true whether the goal is to become chief executive officer or merely to get the boss off one's back. Like many truths, however, this one leaves a lot unsaid. It appears to take the manager off the hook in the employee development process by creating the impression that the "good" ones are going to do it by themselves, and not much can be done to help the rest. What the statement overlooks is the tremendous influence the manager, on behalf of the organization, exerts in the form of opportunities provided or denied for "self" development. It is dangerous to assume that even the most highly motivated achievers in an organization will single-handedly be able to create all the opportunities they need to grow to their full capacity. Employee development is better perceived as a partnership, and the manager who fails to perform his or her share of the job may find some of the best employees going elsewhere for their opportunities.

Even when they accept their share of responsibility, many managers feel that they have done their part in the employee or manager development process when they have authorized an employee with high potential to attend a training program. Such programs often have titles that imply that they are synonymous with management development. Training, or the teaching of new skills, is a legitimate and important part of development, but it does not deserve the blind faith many managers put in it as the solution to all or even most performance problems. Before considering training, it is necessary first to determine whether the performance gap is the result of physical or psychological obstacles that the manager or the organizational climate may have put in the path of the employee. This, of course, is the function of the progress review—to discuss these types of problems openly and to make plans to eliminate them.

Corrective action resulting from the typical progress review is likely to be (1) the removal of obstacles and the reallocation of resources by the manager, (2) specific action taken on new ideas generated during the review session, and (3) steps taken by the employee within the limits of *current* capabilities. Improvement that results from the review itself is for the most part limited to making better use of present capabilities, e.g., getting the employee to do things differently, or changing the conditions so that they allow the employee to use present skills and abilities more effectively.[1]

The progress review may provide indications that training is needed, or of some latent strength that should be nurtured. However, its problem-solving, action-oriented aim is not best suited for developing a career plan designed to move the employee to the new levels of capability that will be needed to do the job over a longer period of time.

The performance appraisal provides the needed focus on personal and professional development, both for growth on the present job and in preparation for future career responsibilities. This unit will review briefly the many things that managers and employees can do, together or separately, to aid the development process. Training is

---

[1]Sometimes, in spite of the manager's best efforts to remove obstacles and motivate the employee, performance remains stubbornly below the level of capability. Mager and Pipe have developed a format for analyzing these situations, based on the relative psychological payoffs for performance and nonperformance. See Robert F. Mager and Peter Pipe, *Analyzing Performance Problems* (Belmont, Calif.: Fearon Publishers, 1970).

one of them. But we will focus mainly on two other concepts that we have found to be especially important to manager development—coaching and delegation.

WORK, CLIMATE, AND INDIVIDUAL

Many tools are available to the manager and the employee for executing their personal development partnership. These have been placed by management development authority Marion Kellogg[2] in three categories: (1) those which put development opportunities into the *work itself,* (2) those which provide a *climate* in which growth is stimulated, and (3) those which are directed at the *individual.*

The Work Itself

A great deal has been written about "job enrichment" as a way to motivate employees. The enriched job offers motivation from increased responsibility, a more comprehensive task that provides feedback on results as well as relief from boredom, and the thrill of achievement that results from completing a meaningful piece of work. All these are a part of, or conducive to, the development of the employee. The design of the job itself is therefore a powerful development tool.

An individual's responsibility should be clearly spelled out in the job description. It is advisable, however, to leave some flexibility in the design and specifications of the job so that the incumbent, as he or she grows in the job, can make of it something which did not exist before. Individuals should be encouraged to operate within broadly defined limits, which must of course be specified to avoid overlap between functions. As the employee tackles increasingly difficult objectives, the job classification must be reviewed and a higher salary range assigned, reflecting the greater contribution to the organization. It is not always possible to promote a person in order to provide a development challenge (nor even to retain those whose skills may outgrow those needed by the organization). Growth within a broadly designed job is therefore a necessary alternative.

---

[2]Marion S. Kellogg, *Closing the Performance Gap* (New York: AMA, 1967), chap. 2.

There are other ways to put development opportunities into the work environment. Special assignments such as task force leadership, trouble shooting, and project team assignments all provide opportunities for your promising employees. Positions such as "Assistant to" create difficulties in assigning responsibility and accountability, and are frowned upon by many managers as costly excess baggage. But, properly controlled, these positions can also be very effective as development assignments. For example, they provide an excellent situation in which the important coaching relationship (described below) can be carried out.

A wise but cynical manager once said, "An organization, or an individual, will only be as good as it (he or she) has to be!" If you include expected standards of performance in the job description,[3] a statement of high expectations can be a powerful development tool in itself. We could argue, of course, that this means of motivating belongs under the "climate" category, but your management climate should be reflected in the design and specification of the job in every way possible.

The Work Climate

The climate in which a person works is composed of all the physical and psychological influences that impinge on the worker in the process of getting the job done. (The psychological forces can even continue to affect a worker off the job, as memories of pleasant or unpleasant work encounters or events come back, or anxiety about that forthcoming sales call or budget review builds up tension.) The organizational environment or climate includes dozens of variables, but the employee's manager is probably the single most powerful influence. We will confine our treatment of climate to the manager (to *you*) and to your role in employee development.

Kellogg subdivides the manager's role in development into categories that reflect (1) the manager's work, (2) attitudes and specific

---

[3]A job description (see Fig. 7) is an extremely useful tool in any management system. In addition to establishing a broad framework within which an employee may grow, its responsibility statements are the basis for setting standards of performance and establishing specific objectives. These become the basis of performance appraisal. These relationships are shown on the Work Planning Guide, Fig. 5. The design of job descriptions is discussed further in Vol. I.

actions toward employee development, and (3) interactions with employees.

The manager's *attitude toward his or her own work* exerts a tremendous effect on the employee's attitude, and hence—for better or worse—on the development of the employee's full potential. Whether the manager cares about it or not, or whether he or she even realizes it, the effect is still there. The manager is a model for employee behavior. It is to the credit of many employees that they reject the manager as a model and go their own way when the model is one they clearly dislike. But this is an extremely chancey approach to employee development, and you will find it worthwhile to do a bit of self-assessment in this respect. What sort of work ethic do you project to your employees? Do you model helpful behavior for subordinate managers? Do you see them doing the same for their employees? Do you project a cautious or a risk-taking image? Do you model collaboration with your manager peers, or do you cue your subordinates that dog-eat-dog competition is the cardinal rule of survival? Do your words and actions reflect loyalty to your organization and its purposes? Remember, little brother is watching you!

Your *attitudes toward employee development* must obviously have an effect also, for example, as they are reflected in your willingness to continue your own education—and, of course, in the priority that you give to helping others develop. Your *expectations* have a big influence on employee performance; what you expect of them in the way of self-development will be a major determinant.

In the end, your organization's capacity for utilizing the new potential that you have encouraged in your people may turn out to be the limiting factor. There will always be a question in the employee-oriented organization as to whether "we are emphasizing employee development to the extent that we are just getting them ready for somebody else." These concerns may reflect the fact that you are raising false expectations in your employees, and emphasize the wisdom of stressing growth in the *present* job first (and growth of the job itself, as we indicated earlier).

All the above are important aspects of the manager's style—the pattern of his or her personal interaction with employees and probably the greatest single influence the manager has on the development climate. We have previously discussed other aspects of managerial style—feedback, support, the sharing of information, all of which are important elements of your pattern of interaction, and we will return to the equally vital topic of delegation/coaching. But first we will discuss briefly the third category of developmental methods, those directed at the individual.

Accent on the Individual

This category includes the various attempts to change the individual rather than the job or the climate in which the person works. Among these attempts are the many types of training we can provide the employee. The hope is that at least some of the training will be translated into changed behavior on the job. Supplementing formal training are the measures taken by the individual himself — for example, attempts to sharpen management skills by taking on leadership roles in community activities. (There is no better way to test and develop your management ability than to take on the task of managing a volunteer activity, where no badge of authority or financial incentive is available to assist you in motivating others.)

First, however, the employee must receive some inputs to awaken awareness of the *need* for training. You provide much of this input through the performance appraisal process itself — through feedback on job performance, and through the many opportunities that day-to-day appraisal, progress reviews, and annual performance appraisal sessions offer to encourage the employee to explore the need for improvement. For the employee to accept training it is often necessary to pave the way. There is nothing more frustrating and unproductive — for the trainee, the manager, or the instructor — than training done under duress.

While the appraisal process provides the opportunity to determine the employee's development needs, the action plans that follow are influenced heavily by the manager's initiative in making available to employees the developmental resources inside or outside the organization. If you do not have internal management development specialists who can provide or recommend professional counseling, testing, and self-awareness training, you should make yourself familiar with outside sources. Another way to facilitate employee self-development is an organizational policy which allows educational leave of absence, released time for training, and/or tuition refund for successful completion of courses.

Two types of self-analysis which are more or less in current vogue, and which deserve special mention, are *laboratory training* (which goes under the names also of T-group, sensitivity, or personal growth training) and *management style analysis* (the most popular of which is called *managerial grid training*). The first of these is especially useful for developing awareness of the effect that habitual behavior patterns can have on the people with whom one interacts,[4] and for providing an opportunity to practice more productive interaction. This can be especially helpful to an employee who has persistent difficulty in dealing effectively with coworkers or who seems particularly resistant or insensitive to the manager's attempts to provide feedback and help.

The grid approach to the assessment of management style is based on an analysis of the degree to which the manager is concerned (1) with his or her *people* as the focus of the management job, and (2) with getting the job done by concentration on the *task*. When the strengths of these two concerns (called, respectively, *people orientation* and *production orientation*) are determined by a self-administered test, and are plotted as the two independent variables on a two-dimensional grid, their relative values determine the manager's position on the grid, which in turn defines his or her style.[5] Some theorists hold that there is one best style, or position on the grid. Our feeling is that the most productive style is determined by the specific situation, and furthermore that it is possible for any style to be effective or ineffective, depending on who is using it.

These are only two of the more commonly offered methods of self-assessment. We have selected them to illustrate that caution is indicated in prescribing *any* such measures too broadly or interpreting the results too rigidly. We do not wish to imply, however, that you should not consider them carefully for possible use in certain cases. A full treatment of these and similar assessment tools is outside the scope of this volume, as is even a superficial coverage of the

---

[4]This type of training was originally, and is still occasionally, carried out in a work group made up, for example, of a manager and his or her "direct reports." Most organizations have found, however, that the insights can be more useful and less threatening when the training takes place with a group of strangers, with whom the trainee can feel freer to try out new behavior patterns and who in turn will feel freer to give more open and honest feedback.

[5]The subsequent training program is usually carried out in a work group with the manager and subordinates, all of whom have completed the style analysis individually. The group then attempts to work out a collective style that will lead to improved organizational effectiveness.

multitude of training courses, devices, tools, and programs available. The self-instructional individual study in which we are together engaged is but one example.[6]

DELEGATION/ COACHING: AN ONGOING PROCESS

We previously cited the delegation/coaching process (these two terms are so closely related that we will consider them as one) under the "climate" category of developmental tools. You may make an equally strong case for considering this process as part of the design of the work, or as a type of individualized training. We wouldn't argue with you if you chose to do either. The importance of the delegation/coaching process is so great that it has effects in all three of these developmental areas — which is the reason we are returning to it for a closer look.

The mythology of management is filled with lurid tales of companies that went down the drain because the chief executive officer, insulated from reality, was doggedly making all major decisions, while frustrated minions tried to carry out the boss's vain wishes and misguided edicts. There have been cases like this, as an examination of recent business publications will confirm. But they are far outnumbered by examples of *over*delegation, the real problem facing managers at all levels of an organization.

At the corporate level, the situation is perhaps better described as overdecentralization than as overdelegation, but the effect is the same. Failure to establish limits of authority (and a lack of appreciation of the other basic principles of delegation) can lead to loss of control, misdirected efforts, frustration of the delegatee, and, at the corporate level, even near-disaster for management and shareholders alike.

The basic problem is that delegation too often is considered as an *act* rather than as an ongoing *process*. We have added the concept of "coaching" to it, because of the strong analogy between effective delegation in a managerial setting and coaching, in say, professional football. The coach, like the manager, owes his success to the performance of the players; the coach can certainly

---

[6]Much of what you have covered in this volume — and in Vols. I and II if you have read them — can be put to broader use in your organization by following the recommendations and procedures described in the *Leader's Manual* that accompanies the series. If you are going to introduce MBO to your organization, the *Leader's Manual* will help you direct the implementation effort.

be said to have delegated tremendous responsibility to the team. In operation, however, the coach is always available to the team; the quarterback is constantly alert for advice from the coach, while the coach is continually observing directly, or analyzing reports of happenings not within his field of vision, and is free with advice when he feels it is warranted. For the coach, delegation is not an action taken and then forgotten, but a continual process. It must be for the manager, too.

Before we describe the process in detail, we refer you to Fig. 9

You are practicing the delegation/coaching process effectively when

You have selected the proper delegatee in terms of qualifications, characteristics and capabilities

You are certain you are not delegating what cannot be delegated

You are not delegating the overall *responsibility* or *accountability*

You have created in the delegatee the sense of responsibility for the job

You have clearly established goals and objectives for the job and made sure the delegatee understands

You and the delegatee understand the aspects of the job that are not being delegated

You are giving the delegatee the authority needed to make the greatest possible contribution to the job

You and the delegatee understand the standards of performance required

You and the delegatee have established checkpoints at which progress is to be reviewed

You are willing to accept methods other than those you might have used to do the job yourself

You have assessed the impact of probable errors or schedule slippages and provided for them

You have encouraged independence

You have arranged for support for the delegatee when needed

You are giving recognition and rewards for good performance

You are providing training and/or coaching where performance is not up to standard

You are not letting the delegatee "hang him- or herself" but have established mutual trust

FIGURE 9

---

for a checklist of conditions that prevail when delegation is being carried out with full effectiveness. If you can rate yourself "satisfactory" on all of them, you are an excellent delegator and should skip the remainder of this unit. (Don't overlook the exercises at the end, however.)

The Ground Rules of Delegating

1. *Select well.* No set of rules alone will make you a successful delegator or coach. Without having sound material with which to work you are nowhere! Use discretion in assigning the critical tasks; keep them yourself if you are not sure of your delegatee's stability, maturity, or ability to "hack it" — or be prepared to devote extra effort to the coaching task.

2. *Don't delegate what is yours.* Some duties and responsibilities are yours and yours alone — including the job of appraising your subordinates and the responsibility for rewarding, disciplining, and coaching them, and seeing to their development. This is not a "personnel job!"

3. *You retain the accountability.* The manager who breathes a sigh of relief after assigning an important task to a subordinate, feeling that the burden is somehow shared, is not on firm ground. Of course the employee is bearing the load, and you can take action, rightly or wrongly, if he or she fails — but if *your* boss is on the ball, you had better not make a practice of this. You create accountability in the employee, but you can't get rid of it! The only sound reason for breathing a sigh of relief is that you have followed these guidelines and done a good job of selection.

4. *Create the feeling of responsibility.* Although you still retain the full responsibility, you must be sure that the employee is aware of the true importance of the assignment — not only to the organization, but to the employee's self-development and future.

5. *Make the objectives clear.* We won't belabor the need to set objectives in any undertaking. In this situation there may be less room for *joint* objective setting. The objective is yours; the employee is being asked to take it over and carry it out. If the true objective is to test the employee, then make this clear.

6. *Make clear what is being withheld.* There may be critical limits, for example, on the allowable cost overrun, beyond which you cannot let the employee go without the risk of losing control. These will be mostly a matter of common sense, but it is easy to give a "gung-ho" young achiever the impression that there are no holds barred in getting the job done.

7. *Assign the authority to get the job done.* The hackneyed advice, "delegate authority commensurate with responsibility" doesn't help much. Delegate enough authority to take the job as far as you think it should be taken without checking with you. Consider the limits on contractual or legal commitments, expenditures, commitment of your department's resources, and the important difference between the *authority to decide* and the *responsibility to initiate, advise, or recommend.*

8. *Agree on standards of performance.* Objectives involve quality, quantity, cost, benefit, and timeliness. Be certain that the assigned task is accompanied by standards for allowable levels on all these factors, where appropriate, just as you would do in setting any objective.

9. *Establish checkpoints.* These can be set at time intervals, at various amounts of expenditure of money or manpower, or at certain specific milestone events or subtask completions. Whichever you choose, tailor the schedule of checks to the needs and ability of the subordinate and to the risk to the organization.

10. *Delegate the "what," not the "how."* There is a great difference between delegating and simply giving instructions. "How" is certainly important, but if one of your purposes is to develop employee capability, observing how will reveal a lot more than telling how, and encourage a lot more creativity. Observing how a person tackles problems, copes with the unexpected, and elicits cooperation from others is especially important in assessing managerial potential.

11. *Assess the risks and provide for them.* Some management pundits solemnly proclaim that a productive organizational climate encourages people to make errors. What nonsense! One serious error in judgment can do irrevocable harm to an organization and to the person who perpetrated it — to say nothing of his or her manager. If your analysis shows this kind of risk associated with a delegated task, limit the risk by reducing the delegatee's decision-making authority, adding more checkpoints, and doing a closer job of coaching — or don't delegate at all! There *will* be failures, but do your best to make sure they are not the result of unsuspected or poorly assigned risks. Turn errors into learning experiences instead of meting out punishment.

12. *Encourage independent action.* Make clear that you expect creative, independent thought by indicating your readiness to help and advise, but only on request. Properly established checkpoints will ensure against pride getting in the way of asking.

13. *Arrange for support.* Most likely the support will be from you. This is the heart of the coaching process, and you should budget your time to be available when your delegatee needs you.

14. *Give recognition when deserved.* Reward not only the completion of the task but also any signs of growth in decision-making ability, independent thought, intelligent risk taking, and even recognition of the need for help. Prompt feedback of your positive reaction to these desirable behaviors will increase your chances of getting more of them.

15. *Take action when things go wrong.* If expectations, commitments, or standards are not being met, first make sure the ground rules are understood by the delegatee. As a last resort, retract authority for whatever portions of the job appear outside his or her capabilities, or for the whole job in serious situations of nonperformance. Assess the possibility of training as a long-range measure to increase competence, or of giving lesser assignments to build confidence.

16. *Develop trust.* If your employee shows signs of reluctance to assume the responsibility for a delegated task, it may be caused by mistrust of your intentions. This is best handled by example, that is, by acting in a manner that will eliminate the doubts and fears. *Prove* that you are willing and ready to help your delegatee develop and to give him or her proper credit for the success of the endeavor. Make it clear that you regard employee development as one of your major responsibilities.

The coaching/delegation process is obviously a continuing and a demanding one, in terms of the time and the interpersonal skill required. Its success depends heavily on the judgments you make about the people you select as delegatees. You will not always pick winners, but by paying attention to all aspects of the appraisal process, day by day, and at intervals in your review procedures, you will get a good reading on which employees are worth the heavy investment in time and effort, and on whom you can depend to carry out your major projects.

We have talked about delegation as if it were a very special activity limited to high-potential employees and their development programs. Actually, of course, we begin delegating the minute we admit that one person can't do everything, and subdivide the organizational mission into doable packages of work.[7] In fact, we can even go so far as to say that running an organization *is* the continuing

---

[7]Some organizations make a clear statement of delegated authority a part of the job description itself. See Fig. 7, Section III.

process of delegation. The principles we have stated, therefore, are general principles of management, and are reemphasized here because of their importance in employee development and in the whole performance appraisal process. We have tried to place delegation in perspective by showing you that it is not just a way of lightening the manager's load and putting the decision-making authority closer to the scene of the action, but a powerful tool in assessing and developing the potential of your human resources.

We conclude our guided tour through the performance appraisal process in the next unit with some comments on compensation and its place in an MBO system—and try to answer the 64-dollar question of how and whether performance appraisal affects performance itself.

EXERCISE 8A Make an inventory of the various developmental tools available to you within your organization and in the surrounding community for use in helping your employees (or yourself in your personal development program). Try using the Work/Climate/Individual categorization.

Work-related Development Aids

Climate-related Aids

Individual-oriented Aids

Commentary on Exercise 8A Your list will be a function of your organization and the surrounding environment, but here are a few opportunities you may have overlooked, or may wish to consider for possible use or investigation.

Work-related Development Aids

Project manager positions
Rotation among training assignments
"Team-at-the-top" management
Vacation replacement pool
Long-range planning team assignments
Good-will ambassador
Rotating chairmanship of staff meetings
MBO implementation coordinator
Employee suggestion review board

Climate-related Aids

Team-building sessions (group sharing of perceptions, with outside facilitator)
Confrontation meetings (face-to-face attitude surveys)
Employee information meetings
Negotiation of objectives
Skip-level meetings (exposure to higher-level management)

Individual-oriented Aids

Programmed instruction
Community college teaching assignment
Toastmasters club
Sales effectiveness training
AMA certification curricula
Transactional analysis program
Assessment center inputs
Educational sabbatical
Public television courses
Management simulation games
Case study and analysis
Career counseling center

EXERCISE 8B   Select from the following situations and play roles as instructed in Exercise 7, with or without an observer.

Situation 1   Retake the roles described in Situation 1 of Exercise 7, using as the basis for your discussion the full spectrum of possibilities for self-development and manager-assisted development that appear in Unit 8.

Situation 2   Do the same kind of retake using Situation 2 of Exercise 7 as your starting point.

Situation 3   Terry Mason is one of your most promising employees. As a management systems analyst, Terry has demonstrated a high degree of ability to understand a new situation and its technology in a short time, and has impressed managers in the various components by the soundness of proposals on streamlining work flow, by establishing new procedures and by using the computer intelligently to provide essential real-time measurements without burying them in printout. This employee's awareness of management's problems combined with a pleasing personality have led you to appoint Terry as leader of an interdepartmental task force to study and make recommendations on the company's quality assurance effort. Quality control now consists mainly of inspecting incoming raw materials and the finished product before it is released to the warehouse for distribution. Recent consumer protection concerns and customer complaints have indicated that a broader effort is necessary, at all points in the marketing, product design, and distribution areas, as well as during manufacture. For example, products are being recommended by the sales force for the wrong applications, products are being designed to meet fuzzy or incomplete specifications, shelf-life control is inadequate, and the manufacturing people feel that they are taking the rap without justification in many cases.

   In addition to Terry, the task force will include representatives at the specialist (nonmanagerial) level who are intimately familiar with the above activities — from field sales headquarters, customer service, warehousing, product engineering, and market development. Staffing of the task force is your responsibility, with the help of the other managers involved. They have nominated their representatives, but you have not yet announced how you intend to provide the leadership.

Terry is understandably a little concerned about acting in this way as leader of a peer group with no formal authority, but you feel that this is an excellent opportunity to demonstrate and encourage the management potential that you feel is there. You have agreed to be the "coach" in this situation, remaining on the sidelines but available with advice and assistance on a continual basis for the duration of the study, which is to be completed in 3 months.

Terry has a lot of questions to ask about how to proceed, especially about the "real" authority the position will have and how to use it most effectively. You anticipate a healthy two-way flow of ideas and questions as the two of you sit down to discuss the job 2 weeks before the start of the study.

Commentary on Exercise 8B

Situations 1 and 2 The observer's checklists that follow Exercise 7 and the commentary on Exercise 8A will provide ample guidance on what you should have covered in these discussions.

Situation 3 This is a coaching/delegation situation into which most readers can put themselves. You may already have gone through something similar either as the manager or the delegate. If so, as you rotated the roles with your partner or partners, you should have shared with one another the advice you have found useful in such situations in your organization.

Whether or not you have been involved in this task force leadership role before, you will find it helpful to review Figure 9 at this point. How well did you score against the ground rules of good delegation?

UNIT 9

THE APPRAISAL PROCESS AND INDIVIDUAL MOTIVATION

MONETARY AND NONMONETARY REWARDS

It is fairly clear that a results-oriented system of management like MBO— pursued with diligence and competence by managers at all levels— can lead to improved results or help to maintain results at a high level for the organization. It is less clear how or even whether a comprehensive approach to performance appraisal can contribute significantly to individual performance. Many managers believe that the *objectives* provide all the necessary direction or impetus, and that once the action plans have committed the necessary resources, all that is required to keep things moving is a monthly report to management on the progress to date—backed up by whatever action management must take to see that any slippages are made up.

If that kind of action *is* taken by management, you will have a working MBO system of sorts, and in fact one that will work quite well in a strongly directive management climate. Often however, the follow-up action is not taken effectively, the loop is not closed, and another organization is added to the ranks of those who tried MBO, "but it didn't do anything for us."

The question remains — does the appraisal function serve only to close the MBO loop and provide a more finely tuned directive force, or does it through some magic of its own strengthen the motivation of the individual just because he or she is being appraised? The question is not an idle one, nor do we mean to set up a straw man in asking it. The history of the appraisal process contains too many cases of failure and disappointment for us to present our recommendations as the key to employee motivation. We do make the obvious claim that encouraging and guiding an employee through a formal appraisal process is likely to result in the employee's developing competence in important areas over the long term.

We can also claim, without serious challenge, that the problem-solving discussions that take place during the progress reviews provide a programmed opportunity (and responsibility) for the manager to remove obstacles from the path of the employee. This opportunity, if properly exploited, can be used to improve the performance level over the immediate term.

APPRAISAL AND MOTIVATION

But what is the effect on the many employees who have limited growth potential and who have difficulty in spite of the manager's assistance? And what of highly competent employees who can solve their work problems alone and need little encouragement or help in their self-development? Does the appraisal process do anything to improve the performance of these people, and if so, how?

To get at the answers to those questions, let's consider what the appraisal process produces in the way of outputs. For the employee, it provides confirmation of a job well done and personal awareness of needs for improvement if the job is not well done. In either case, the employee is provided with new goals and objectives. The approval of the manager provides positive recognition from an important person in the life of the employee. Finally, by stressing personal growth and development, the process gives the employee a strong boost along the road to self-actualization. For those who are highly motivated by the need for achievement, recognition, and self-actualization, a positive appraisal can provide a number of rewards, and it is reasonable to believe that such individuals will work hard in the pursuit of worthwhile objectives to be sure that they continue to receive these rewards. Sometimes, persons who have high levels of need in the three areas mentioned above are lacking in the ability required to reach their objectives. For these people, increased awareness of their deficiencies, and tailoring of objectives to provide continual stretch can serve as a positive stimulus to improve. This stimulus is supplied by the performance appraisal.

At the other end of the scale are employees who are capable, but, for sometimes unfathomable reasons, appear to be motivated best by close supervision and constant prodding. We hope that you are not excessively burdened with this type of employee, but even in such cases the frequent review and objective-setting process can provide evidence that somebody cares about performance and is willing to give extra time and attention to seeing that it is obtained — against objectives that are set jointly, if possible, or *imposed* if not.

Within the limits of present-day motivation theory, therefore, performance appraisal has a potentially positive effect on performance, whether employees are highly or poorly motivated, or of average or high capability. You will have a difficult time measuring that effect, but you may be assured that it is there!

THE ROLE OF MONEY IN MOTIVATION

Even in this enlightened age, most people work principally for money. Money is a complex motivator, serving as a goal object that satisfies a number of psychological needs. These needs may relate to security or the desire for creature comforts that only money can satisfy. In some cases, the pursuit and accumulation of money have seemingly become rewards in themselves, even though security and goods are no longer an issue. In these cases, the money may be just a symbol to provide the recognition and self-esteem that are the real needs. Money may also be the indication self-motivated achievers need to confirm their perception that their performance is truly substantial. Whatever need money satisfies, if a money-motivated individual perceives that the level of salary — or the amount of a raise — is related to the amount of work done, he or she will tend to produce more. To the extent that the performance appraisal supports, justifies, and is used intelligently in awarding a salary increase, it helps to stimulate higher performance.

Of course, you should not expect a very favorable review followed by an average increase to be especially motivating, any more than you would expect a poor review followed by an average increase to solve any problems. If money is to be a true motivator, the rewards must differentiate between good and poor performance.

MONEY AND THE APPRAISAL PROCESS

We acknowledge the fact that the appraisal process is commonly used to decide who gets salary increases and how much. By this time, we hope we have convinced you that the process can serve more important purposes — loop closing, problem solving, employee development, and creating a more productive personal relationship between managers and their employees. Nevertheless, the manager needs all the inputs he or she can find in making the important salary decision, and the single most fertile source is the appraisal process — its critical incident files, records of objectives and action plans and progress reviews, and the overall performance appraisal document itself all provide valuable data. But in spite of this wealth of data, the MBO approach to performance appraisal has failed to live up to its promise of quantifying what had previously been pretty much a matter of a manager's judgment. With the exception of some work situations in which output can be counted — and in which the same type of output characterizes the work of more than one person in the same component so that performances can be compared — a manager must still resort to judgment in deciding how to slice the salary-increase pie. We make that flat statement in the hope that it will challenge your thinking in an area that needs much more study.

The state of the art is expressed well by Dr. Nathan Winstanley, a practitioner in the field, who recommends[1] that formal appraisal be taken out of the salary administration process, that automatic merit increases be given up to the midpoint of a salary range on a probationary "go-no go" basis, and that the upper half of the range be reserved for those demonstrating exceptional work. To implement this, he also recommends that a portion of the money allocated to a component for salary increases be withheld from the "automatic"

[1]Nathan B. Winstanley, "The Use of Performance Appraisal in Compensation Administration," The *Conference Board Record,* vol. 12, no. 3, pp. 43–47, March 1975.

category and used to reward those completing an outstanding piece of work. He suggests further that an arbitrary guideline of some sort is necessary in making such awards — for example, 85 percent of the employees should be placed in the "competent" category, with the remainder categorized as either "exceptional" or "marginal." Only the exceptional would receive merit rewards.

We do not agree with Winstanley that the appraisal process should be divorced from the salary determination, because if carried out as we have described, that process is obviously the best way to sharpen the manager's judgment in making salary decisions. We are still heavily reliant, however, on the manager's judgment as to what constitutes outstanding or exceptional performance, or what qualities or accomplishments define the exceptional employee.

THE IMPORTANCE OF SALARY ADMINISTRATION

We described earlier some special situations in which money genuinely appeared to be a motivator. For the most part, however, pay is perceived by the employee as a "deserved" reward and, as Frederick Herzberg found,[2] a person's pay is more likely to act as an irritant or a "dissatisfier" than as a motivator. The failure of many industrial shop incentive pay plans attests to the complex and sometimes negative effect that money exerts on the motivation to work.

Much of the problem is a result of what employees perceive as inequity between themselves and other persons or groups with whom they compare themselves. Prerequisite to removing this irritation is a pay and job classification plan that makes sense to the employee, and will in turn allow pay to exert whatever motivation it may have in a particular situation.

The first step in preparing such a plan is to ensure that there is internal equity, that is, the difference in rates for any two positions is defensible in terms of the responsibilities, the experience and education required, and so on. The second step is to assure that your positions have external equity with similar positions in comparable organizations in your labor market area. This is probably even more important in an employee's mind than internal equity. Accountant A

---

[2]See Frederick Herzberg, *Work and the Nature of Man* (Cleveland: World, 1966), pp. 125–126.

in your firm is likely to have more information about the pay of Accountant B in another firm than about Accountant C in another component of your own organization. Furthermore, if there is inequity externally, it can affect whole classes of employees and lead to the loss of good workers to other firms, while internal comparisons may be limited to one individual and may lead merely to a request for an internal transfer rather than to a total loss to your organization.

Your best efforts to ensure equity through your salary administration plan will still not provide the final answer to salary complaints. For example, the best possible plan will not prevent inflation from becoming an issue. Complaints about inflation are very difficult to deal with, especially for middle managers who in some respects may be even bigger victims than their employees. But if employees see that others on the outside are similarly affected, at least you are on even terms with your competitors.[3]

Salary compression is another difficult internal equity issue. This term refers to the steadily decreasing salary differential between a professional or managerial employee with 15 to 20 years of experience and a new hire, fresh out of college.

For practice, you may wish to try taking the role of a manager explaining to a subordinate accounting manager with 15 years of experience earning $24,000 per year why a new and green MBA accounting major has just been hired at $16,000 per year. (Hint: First establish in your own mind to what degree one should pay for potential as well as for performance, but don't blame us if the argument backfires when you try to use it!) This perceived disparity can become a crucial equity issue if your competitors have taken steps to correct such situations and you have not. The loss of 20 years of experience can be devastating.

---

[3]It may not be possible for a town or city government to achieve dollar equity with similar positions in industry in its locality, or for a university to pay its managers what they might earn in industry. Nonfinancial incentives must make up a substantial part of the difference, however, if the balance is to be maintained. Such incentives are easier to provide in a university environment; a city may have to settle for a dynamic balance in which it is continually "training good people for industry," or a static balance in which it becomes saddled with a progressively inferior work force. The latter trend is, of course, counter to the increasing demands on local government for more sophisticated decision making and improved services at lower cost.

"BUT WE DON'T HAVE A MERIT PAY PLAN"

Managers in organizations that do not have a merit pay plan often resist the idea of performance appraisal as a motivator, feeling that positive feedback to the employee will serve only to emphasize the lack of a financial reward, and in effect amount to rubbing salt in the wound. Such problems are common in the management of hourly rated employees, for whom pay progression is fixed, and often mandatory at time intervals defined by a union contract or by company policy. The very idea of MBO with its complications—joint objective setting, merit raise decisions, and all the rest—is looked upon either as not warranted by the situation or as a threat to union-management relations.

We agree that an organization should give a lot of thought to it before attempting to install MBO in the shop. The first priority is to make certain that the concepts are fully understood and working among all the levels of management, first-line included, before taking the system further.[4] However, there are advantages to an MBO appraisal system, even when MBO as a total concept is not deemed applicable and the appraisal and the pay of an employee are apparently unrelated.

In shop organizations or components that have not converted to a merit system, a manager usually has latitude to *withhold* an automatic progression increase for less than satisfactory performance. Negative incentives are not generally as effective as positive rewards in improving performance, but they can be helpful in dealing with a marginal employee, provided the manager stresses the need for improvement and presents objectives to be met by the employee in order to get back on the salary progression track.

For a shop employee motivated by higher-level needs, the appraisal process has a lot to offer in terms of the benefits discussed earlier. After all, decisions on candidates for promotion still have to be made, based on the assessment of potential, and development of their potential is still a matter of great interest to many people. The failure of managers—in or out of the shop—to use all available tools to recognize, develop, and reward potential in their employees is harmful both to the employee and to the organization.

---

[4]We discuss this at greater length in Unit 7 of Vol. II.

RATER BIAS   A concern that has always existed about performance appraisal is the inequitable distribution of rewards—salary included—that may occur when one manager is very demanding in terms of objectives and performance, and another is an "easy" rater.[5] The answer to this problem lies in the MBO process itself. If the keynote is improved performance, and the overall objectives are set by a competent top level of management, each successive level will be held accountable for its commitments in support of the total effort. Any weak links in the management chain will be quickly identified. One sure way to become a weak link is to fail to set tight objectives or to attempt to gloss over mediocre performance by giving outstanding appraisals.

As with any system, however, there are ways to beat the MBO system—and in most organizations you will find people who are out to do so. Some of them will be very creative, and their efforts difficult to detect. For the most part, however, such systemic failures can be traced to inattention or lack of concern on the part of the system monitors, that is, failure of the control function, of which the appraisal process is such an important part. Make no mistake about

---

[5] Some organizations find that pooled judgments—multiple ratings by the immediate superior and several other individuals closely associated with the employee's work—are of some help in avoiding or at least diluting rater bias.

Drawing by
William Hamilton;
© 1977 The New Yorker
Magazine, Inc.

"I'm highly overrated, thank God."

it, MBO is a difficult and demanding kind of management—and the appraisal process is probably its most difficult element. But those who chose management as a profession—as opposed to those who sought it as a status symbol or were thrust into it as a reward—didn't ask for a rose garden, and will, we think, recognize the value of this results-oriented system.

If you have stayed with us this far, you are probably interested in making management a true profession. If so, you have chosen well. As a manager, the way you select your key results areas, with proper attention to customers, clients, suppliers, employees, stockholders, and the public welfare, and the concern and effort you place on continued improvement of results in all these areas, will have a profound impact on the future of our society. Give it all you've got!

156

EXERCISE 9   With a coworker, try placing yourself in the position of the manager or employee in the following situations, as you did in previous exercises. Then swap roles and compare the two approaches and their results.

Situation 1   Your city government has a salary classification plan that assigns a grade level to every position. Each level has six salary steps from bottom (a) to top (f), and seniority is the primary determinant of salary level. A cursory annual appraisal system enables the manager to deny a step increase if performance is unsatisfactory. But, with the exception of an occasional firing after a continued spell of non-performance, everyone sooner or later reaches the top step of his or her grade level, and becomes eligible only for occasional cost-of-living increases from then on. The department has a mix of people, including fast movers who reach the top of the salary range rapidly and move on to higher-level jobs, and employees who progress more slowly and have limited potential.

Jay Greenfeld, a sanitary engineer, is a solid contributor, but has limited potential for advancement to higher-level jobs. An employee of the department for 9 years, Jay reached the top (step f) of grade 7 last year, and is eligible on the first of next month only for a cost-of-living adjustment of 4 percent. A younger engineer, who is acknowledged to be a lower-calibre performer than Jay is scheduled to receive 10.4 percent (4 percent cost-of-living allowance plus 6.4 percent as a one-step increase from base rate a to step b). Loose talk has brought this to Jay's attention. Jay is concerned about the apparent inequity of this situation, feeling that pay is supposed to reflect performance, and he is disturbed at the realization that he may have reached the end of the line as far as adequate raises go, considering the current 5 to 6 percent inflation rate. At Jay's request, he is about to discuss this situation with his department head.

Situation 2*   The general manager of the appliance division of a major electrical manufacturer has just been informed of a new companywide year-

---

*Note: You will find this discussion more productive if both of you take time to make some notes before starting.

end salary incentive plan, which will distribute to the divisions 10 percent of the net profit earned by the company during the year in excess of a certain percentage of the stockholders' equity in the total business. This amount is to be distributed among the divisions in proportion to each division's contribution to the total net profit.

The company comptroller has authorized each division manager to divide up the bonus at his or her discretion — with the stipulation, however, that all management personnel (including plant supervisors and key technical and professional personnel who are not strictly considered managers) are to be considered eligible to receive a portion. The appliance division will receive $187,000 to be distributed with the February paychecks.

The manager has gone through a quick mental rundown of the organization (five departments — manufacturing, marketing, engineering, finance, and employee relations, with a total of 100 management and nonmanagerial employees who should probably be considered eligible) and prudently decided that help was needed! The employee relations department manager has been called on the telephone, and given the ground rules and the nature of the problem. She knocks on the boss's door, still pondering how to allocate $187,000 equitably. There are questions in the ER manager's mind as to the boss's criteria for including approximately 55 nonmanagerial people among the 100, and also how the performance appraisal process can best be used to assure an "objective" distribution.

Commentary on Exercise 9

Forgive us for throwing you these curves. These "impossible" situations, which would tax the wisdom of Solomon, are typical of those you may some day encounter. They challenge the pay-for-performance ideal and also (in the second case) throw serious doubt on the viability of the notion that individual contributions or even larger subsystem results can be quantified or ranked for the purposes of determining rewards.

Your discussion of Situation 1 should have raised the question of *how* the manager judged the employee to have limited potential, and should have provided a little practice in conveying the ultimate bad news to an employee who really has reached the end of the line. We also trust that you spotted the fallacy in confusing the size of a pay increase with the *level* of pay. Finally, we hope that you also asked yourself how it was that Jay didn't seem to be aware of the system of salary administration after such a long time in the organization. Such ignorance on the part of the employee is in itself a problem that the manager should tackle promptly.

The second case illustrates the relative ease with which rewards are distributed when there is a "countable" output, for example, profit dollars for the divisions. (Other examples are sales dollars or contribution-margin dollars for salesmen.) But it gets very difficult, as you found, to compare the contributions of subsystems such as manufacturing and marketing, and even more difficult when you introduce a staff function like employee relations. We won't criticize if you finally decided to divide the bonus among the functions on the basis of the numbers of eligible people, leaving it to the judgment of the functional managers to reward the individuals appropriately. If you decided to follow the advice of Winstanley (see Unit 9), you should have hammered out some guidelines for the whole division on what constitutes "exceptional" performance to cut down on rater bias.

BIBLIOGRAPHY

We have selected the following books as good sources for backup material in the area of performance appraisal, and in several cases for general background and alternative points of view on MBO in general. We have stressed the writings of practitioners and consultants rather than straight academicians because of the hands-on experience that their works reflect.

Banaka, Wm. H.: *Training in Depth Interviewing* (New York: Harper & Row, 1971).

Provides other models for developing a topic in the interview process and contains additional exercises. A good and concise treatment of the psychological issues in interviewing. Of particular interest is an almost word-for-word analysis of what goes on in a lengthy counseling interview.

Drucker, Peter F.: *Management: Tasks, Responsibilities, Practices* (New York: Harper & Row, 1973).

This is probably already on your bookshelf. A very readable distillation of just about everything Drucker has said, it is "must" reading for any manager. Especially pertinent to the performance appraisal process are Chap. 8 on key result areas and multiple objectives in general, Chap. 23 on human resources, Chap. 34 on self-control and measurement, and Chap. 38 on managerial communication. This is a book to consult for concise, authoritative opinion on many subjects. You will want to read it all.

Fein, Mitchell: *Motivation for Work,* Monograph 4 (Norcross, Georgia: American Institute of Industrial Engineers, 1974).

A provocative treatment of motivation by means of incentive pay, based on the thesis that if pay brings people to work in the first place, it should be useful in motivating them to work harder. Valuable for those who want to delve further into the relationship between pay and performance, but be prepared for a strong challenge to your faith in behavioral science.

Gorden, Raymond L.: *Interviewing: Strategy, Techniques and Tactics* rev.ed. (Homewood, Illinois: The Dorsey Press, 1975).

Written primarily to meet the needs of public opinion researchers, the later chapters provide much further information on the interviewing techniques and tactics covered briefly in Unit 7. There are also a number of laboratory exercises which may be helpful in practicing these techniques.

Humble, John W.: *Improving Business Results* (Maidenhead, Berkshire, England: McGraw-Hill, 1968).

A good review of MBO in general, included here as a rich source of ideas on forms (some quite detailed) for use in progress review and performance appraisal. Case histories reflect the usage of this system in Europe.

Kellogg, Marion S.: *Closing the Performance Gap* (New York: AMA, 1967).

The author is the first woman to reach the vice-presidential level in one of our largest corporations, the General Electric Company. Her extensive experience in career planning and the development of human resource potential is passed along in this book, with considerable emphasis on problem situations. She tackles the termination decision with a combination of great sensitivity and firmness.

Kellogg, Marion S.: *What To Do About Performance Appraisal* rev.ed. (New York: AMACOM, 1975).

This revision of an earlier edition pulls together the experience of the writer, a pioneer in the field of MBO and performance appraisal, in implementing and consulting with operating managers on the General Electric system of results-oriented appraisal called Work Planning and Review. Contains many ideas on forms, checklists, and other appraisal tools. An excellent statement of the philosophy of management in an organization to which the growth of human potential is a critical matter.

Lopez, Felix M.: *Evaluating Employee Performance* (Chicago: Public Personnel Association, 1968).

A comprehensive review of the history and methods of performance appraisal published by a public sector association and thus helpful to readers in government organizations, but more broadly applicable as well. The author was manpower development, selection, and placement manager for the Port of New York Authority for many years before entering academic life.

Mager, Robert F., and Peter Pipe: *Analyzing Performance Problems,* or *"You Really Oughta Wanna"* (Belmont, Calif.: Lear-Siegler/Fearon, 1970).

This paperback is an excellent short course on reinforcement theory in changing human behavior, and provides an easy-to-follow model for analyzing performance problems to which training is *not* the answer. It focuses on eliminating the primarily psychological barriers that prevent people from doing as well as they know how, and sheds an interesting light on the manager who, having gone through the analysis, decides not to do anything about it anyhow.

McConkey, Dale D.: *MBO for Non-Profit Organizations* (New York: AMACOM, 1975).

The manager in a nonprofit organization will find in this book many examples of the approaches, emphasis, reporting systems and organizational modifications used by church organizations, universities, government agencies, and hospitals in their initial efforts to install performance-based management systems.

Odiorne, George S.: *Management by Objectives: A System of Managerial Leadership* (New York: Pitman, 1965).

An eminently readable and authoritative book by one of the pioneers of management by objectives. Devotes much more attention to performance appraisal than most general MBO texts.

INDEX

Page numbers in *italic* indicate charts or graphs.